THE BUSINESS GUIDE
TO
CHINA

THE BUSINESS GUIDE
TO
CHINA

Laurence Brahm and Li Dao Ran

Asia, an imprint of

a division of Reed Elsevier (Singapore) Pte. Ltd.
1 Temasek Avenue
#17-01 Millenia Tower
Singapore 039192

ISBN 981 00 7079 9

Cover design by Fred Rose
Typeset by Linographic Services Pte Ltd. (10/12pt New Century Schoolbook)
Printed in Singapore by KHL Printing Co Pte Ltd

ABOUT THE AUTHORS

Li Dao Ran is the deputy director of the Great Wall Economic Law Firm, under the Ministry of Foreign Trade and Economic Cooperation (MOFTEC) of the People's Republic of China, where he specialises in direct foreign investment, arbitration and project financing.

From 1982–1992 Mr Li served as director of MOFTEC's Department of Treaties and Law, where he was actively involved in formulating China's policy regarding the regulation of direct foreign investment and in formulating industry specific policies. He was also involved in the interpretation and application of laws and regulations in these areas.

Mr Li was also a principal drafter of China's laws on Chinese–Foreign Equity Joint Ventures, Chinese–Foreign Cooperative Joint Ventures and Wholly Foreign-owned Investment Enterprises, as well as the implementing regulations pertaining to these laws. He has since been advising on the interpretation of these laws and regulations.

Laurence J. Brahm is managing director of Naga Group Limited, a specialised investment advisory company advising on investments and providing transactional support for multinationals entering and establishing operations in China. He is based in Naga Group's Beijing office, and frequently travels to Naga Group's offices in Shanghai and Hong Kong.

Mr Brahm is a lawyer and political economist by profession. He has been advising on transactions in China for over a decade and specialises in negotiating and structuring joint ventures, financing, and dispute resolution.

Mr Brahm has also written and published extensively on China's monetary reforms, business and investment laws, and economic and political development.

PREFACE

Since opening its doors to foreign investment in 1979, China has undergone tremendous changes, and a legal system for foreign trade and investment has been built up from a virtual void to one that is now one of the most complete legal systems for foreign investment in a developing transitional economy.

The purpose of this book is to provide a broad outline of the legislation and various issues involved in establishing an investment and conducting business activities in the People's Republic of China. While it is impossible to provide complete details of all the legal aspects of this framework within the covers of one book, we have attempted to provide a synopsis of the key issues and a structural composition for understanding how the existing system relating to encouraging and protecting foreign investment and business activities in China works.

Given the rapid developments in China, it is virtually impossible to be able to cover all new legislation — given that such legislation changes nearly every day. Nevertheless, it is our hope that this book will become a basic reference for foreign investors and business people entering the China market.

Laurence J. Brahm
Li Dao Ran

September 1996
Beijing

CONTENTS

PART 1

ECONOMIC REFORM AND INVESTMENT OPPORTUNITIES, AN OVERVIEW

CHAPTER 1

ECONOMIC AND FINANCIAL REFORMS

Upon adopting the four modernisations program in the 1980s, it was Deng Xiaoping's objective to open China's economy to the outside world and quadruple gross national production by the year 2000. One of the most impressive results of the program put into effect by Deng Xiaoping was the attainment of this goal in 1995, when the Chinese gross national production quadrupled to RMB 5,760 billion, five years ahead of target.

In addition to the major macro-economic reforms which involved a number of incentives for foreign investors, some key reforms involved the financial sector. Major transformations of the financial sector in the early 1980s began with taxation reforms, foreign exchange reforms, and eventually a complete overhaul of the entire banking system. The 1990s will see China adopt a system of taxation similar to that in effect in many Western countries, a convertible Renminbi currency, and a modern banking system with the People's Bank of China acting as the central monetary authority.

DEVELOPING A 'SOCIALIST MARKET' ECONOMY

Much of China's economic reform policy guiding the economy's development in the 1990s has been driven by Deng Xiaoping's theory of developing a 'socialist market economy with Chinese characteristics'. This concept recognises the need to introduce market economy principles into overall State policies. The underlying emphasis is to restructure China's economy along lines which are distinctly in tune with the realities and problems of living faced daily by the Chinese people themselves. This has led to many of the economic theories of the West and proselytisations of the World Bank and the International Monetary Fund being thrown to the winds.

The Decision of the Central Committee of the Chinese Communist Party on Issues Concerning the Establishment of a Socialist Market Economy serves as a keystone document for this reform platform. It points out that a socialist market economy requires a healthy macro-control mechanism. 'Macro-control of the economy' allows for growth

3

to be achieved mainly by economic means, within the context of broad-brush centralised macro-planning.

In order to develop China's economy within the context of these policies, short-term major steps have been taken in the fields of finance, taxation, banking and investment, and in the regulatory and planning systems. Mutually coordinated and controlled mechanisms between the various departments of the State involved in planning, banking and finance will lead to better overall control of the country's economic activities and development.

TAXATION SYSTEM REFORMS

Much effort is being devoted to improving the taxation system. The principles underlying the system will achieve:

- uniformity in tax laws;
- fair treatment in taxation;
- simplification of the taxation system; and
- rational division of the tax-levying power.

An intermediate taxation system with Value Added Tax as the principal link is being introduced. A consumption tax is now levied on a limited number of commodities and a business tax continues to be levied on most non-commodity enterprises.

The income tax on State-owned enterprises has been lowered: State-owned enterprises must pay taxes to rationalise relations between the State and State-owned enterprises in the distribution of profits. Meanwhile, the State has stopped allocating funds for major energy and transport projects. The taxes for enterprises and individuals have been unified, tax rates standardised and the base for taxation extended. Some new taxes have been introduced and some existing ones modified. Tax reduction and exemption practices have been examined to close loopholes.

DEVELOPING FINANCIAL MARKETS

To establish a socialist market economy, it is necessary to develop a market system according to the State's macro-control program. State planning control mechanisms play a basic role in the distribution of resources while China's economic development is in a state of transition. In this regard, the present focus is on the development of financial, labour, real estate, technology and information markets.

The development and perfection of the financial markets is being carried out with banks forming the central link. In the capital market, it is necessary to actively and steadily develop financing through bond and stock issues. A primary step will be to establish bond-issuing institutions and a bond credibility assessment system, as a guarantee for the healthy growth of the bond market. The issuing and listing of stocks is likewise being standardised and gradually expanded.

The money market system is also being developed through more extensive inter-bank lending and bill acceptances on discounts. The People's Bank of China, as the central bank, conducts transactions involving State bonds. Financing activities such as fundraising and lending in violation of State regulations are unlawful and strictly prohibited.

RESTRUCTURING OF THE BANKING SYSTEM

Restructuring of the country's banking system is being accelerated. The People's Bank of China independently implements the country's monetary policy under the leadership of the State Council. Whereas the central bank once relied mainly on its control over credit rates, its activities now include:

- the use of the rates on deposit reserves;
- the interest rates on its loans;
- public market business; and
- other types of business.

as a basis for:

- regulating the money supply;
- maintaining the stability of the currency's value;
- supervising the banking institutions; and
- maintaining the banking order.

Business with non-banking institutions will stop. Administration of the banking industry will be kept separate from that of the securities industry. Preparations are under way for the establishment of a monetary policy committee whose task is to make timely readjustment of the country's monetary and credit policies. In recognition of the need for nation-wide circulation yet centralised control of money, branches of the People's Bank of China represent the Bank's headquarters. The Bank is actively providing for the creation of transregional branches.

A computer network will be introduced to serve the entire banking system. The use of commercial bills and drafts and other settlement instruments will be extended. Settlement practice will be placed under strict discipline and become more efficient. Extensive use of credit cards will be encouraged while cash circulation will be drastically reduced.

Policy-implementing banks are to be established; these will be separate from commercial banks. Preparations are being made to establish a State development bank and an import/export credit bank, and to reorganise the Agricultural Bank of China so that it can undertake strictly defined policy-oriented business.

Commercial banks will be further developed: the specialised banks that now exist are to be transformed into commercial banks. Rural and urban cooperative banks are to be established according to demand. Commercial banks operate on the basis of balance sheet ratio management and risk management. Non-banking financial institutions will be standardised and developed.

FOREIGN EXCHANGE REFORMS

The central bank will adjust basic interest rates in the light of the supply and demand of capital, and will allow commercial banks to float their deposit interest rates within a specified range. Control of foreign exchange will be reformed to establish a system of controlled floating exchange rates based on market fluctuations and a foreign exchange market of uniform standard. Efforts are being made to turn Renminbi gradually into a convertible currency. Convertibility, with limited restrictions, began in 1996 through 'capital accounts'.

LOANS FOR INVESTMENT PURPOSES

A system is being introduced slowly to encourage investment by bodies corporate and to assess the risks attached to bank credit loans in various fields of investment. Under this system, enterprises will make independent decisions on investment in competitive projects, and will shoulder the responsibility for the risks involved. The decision to grant loans to finance such investments will be made by the commercial banks on the basis of creditor assessment and risk. The investing enterprises will in turn be responsible themselves for profits and losses. A system to record the registration of investment projects will replace the current system of examination and approval by the relevant administrative authorities. Financing and investment in this respect will gradually move from a system of planning and approval to one where they are wholly governed by market forces. The State will give guidance by means of its industrial policy alone.

CONCLUSION

The reforms of the financial sector are by far the most impressive of the recent reforms which China has implemented. One could say that the developments of the early 1990s were most clearly influenced by the financial sector reform.

China maintains a tight credit policy, which is clearly in the interests of the country. Between 1990 and 1995, national growth averaged 11.5% while inflation was highest at 22%. It is the intention in the second half of the 1990s, beginning in 1996, to bring national growth down to 8% and keep the inflation level below national growth. If this can be achieved, China's financial reforms will bring a new era in the growth of China's economy, moving it from a developing economy to a fully modernised economic superpower.

CHAPTER 2

OPPORTUNITIES AND INCENTIVES

During the 1980s, China sought to adopt an import substitution economic model whereby foreign investment was encouraged particularly in those infrastructure and productive sectors where China needed to effect a complete overhaul. Foreign investment incentives involved tax reductions and exemptions particularly in the coastal regions where Special Economic Zones (SEZs) were established.

The 1990s will see an extension of policies encouraging foreign investment into the interior of China and a redirecting of investment away from non-productive sectors into those sectors which the Chinese economy requires. While it is the general policy to continue to encourage foreign investment, China is now moving into an export promotion economic model whereby investment is encouraged particularly in those sectors which will help China's export. This chapter sets forth an overview of the policies which are currently in effect.

GUIDELINES FOR FOREIGN INVESTMENT

The guidelines for investment by foreign capital are based on a policy of opening wider to the outside world, and actively attracting overseas capital, technology, talent and management experience.

The conditions under which investments can be made and managed will be further improved, the rate of importing foreign capital and technology will be further expanded, fields for investment will be further extended, and the domestic market will be opened further.

The same conditions will apply nationally and administration will be streamlined in accordance with the law. Foreign investors are encouraged to invest in:

- infrastructure projects;
- primary industries;
- high technology;
- the technical transformation of old enterprises; and
- export-oriented production.

Future Investment Areas

China's rich resources and domestic market will further attract foreign capital and technology to boost economic growth. China's industrial policy with regard to foreign investment in the coming years will emphasise the following:

(1) encouragement of investment in agricultural projects for comprehensive development and for export;

(2) a greater ratio of foreign investment in infrastructure construction, primary industry, and capital- and technology-intensive projects and high-tech projects;

(3) encouragement of investment in projects to supplement the production of raw and semi-finished materials, parts and elements for ongoing industrial production;

(4) encouragement of foreign investment in accelerating the technical transformation of existing enterprises, especially investment in the technical transformation of large and medium-sized State-owned enterprises;

(5) continued encouragement of investment in export-oriented manufacturing industry, especially major enterprises in the coastal regions that are technology-intensive;

(6) production of exports with high added value so as to strengthen their competitiveness on the international market;

(7) a rational development of tourist hotels and the real estate industry;

(8) curtailment of excessive growth of service facilities for high consumption; and

(9) a gradual opening, or controlled expansion of the opening, of the banking, commercial material supply, foreign trade, transportation and other trade service industries.

The opening up of the above areas to foreign investment will be done in a controlled and methodical way and on the basis of experience gained in pilot projects.

Investing in Infrastructure Projects

Investment in the construction of infrastructure projects should encourage and attract participation from all quarters. Local governments are responsible for the construction of regional infrastructure projects.

Major national construction projects will be conducted under centralised planning, and financed by the State development banks and other policy-implementing banks through:

- the issuing of financial bonds;
- equity participation;
- loans under preferential policies; and
- other forms of fundraising.

PREFERENTIAL POLICIES

The country's preferential policies to encourage foreign investment will undergo appropriate readjustment. The basic principles will be to:

(1) enable all foreign-funded enterprises in all parts of the country to enjoy the same treatment;

(2) help foreign-funded industries in the open coastal regions to be updated and encourage part of the labour-intensive manufacturing enterprises with foreign investment to move to the central west part of China;

(3) make the industrial policy more favourable to high-tech industry; and

(4) gradually weaken the practice of encouraging foreign investment through preferential tax policies so that a uniform tax policy will apply throughout the country.

The preferential policy of tax reduction and exemption for foreign-funded projects which the State has encouraged will continue in the medium term. Preferential policy will be uniformly applied to industrial projects receiving State encouragement, regardless of differences in geographical location. Preferential treatment will include:

- a prolonged period of enterprise income tax reduction or exemption, and approval for accelerated depreciation of fixed assets;
- priority in the issue of policy-oriented loans;
- arrangement for export quotas and permits; and
- permission for products to be sold mainly on the domestic market with priority in buying foreign exchange.

The preferential policy treatment will be extended to investments which develop inland agriculture and animal husbandry, to projects

11

tapping resources, and to the energy and material industries. This will be accompanied by an appropriate increase in domestic loans in coordination with foreign investment in projects in the central and western regions and provinces, so that a greater part of the products of foreign-funded enterprises will be available to be sold on the domestic market. The central and western provinces and regions will have the authority to approve the setting up of foreign-funded enterprises up to a total investment of US$20 million. Meanwhile, the policies will remain unchanged towards the five SEZs and the various development zones approved by the State. Preferential tax policies will not operate in any new development zones to be approved in the future.

INVESTMENT BY MULTINATIONALS

A major source of foreign capital is investment from multinational corporations. The Ministry of Foreign Trade and Economic Cooperation has put forward seven policy proposals to attract investment in China by multinationals.

(1) Further efforts will be made to assist enterprises to manage their foreign exchange balances through investment from multinationals, so that such enterprises may freely regulate their foreign exchange balances across different regions in the country.

(2) Fields for investment will be extended to include:
   • enterprises partially or solely owned by multinationals that have been established in bonded areas since 1993;
   • retail commerce solely or partially invested by multinationals, beginning on an experimental basis in the five SEZs and part of the open coastal cities (including the power to engage in import/export business for some commodities); and
   • banking, insurance, air transport, consulting services, and financial and accounting services, following relaxation of restrictions.

(3) Permission will be granted for multinationals to set up investment companies in China.

(4) Investments by multinationals will be encouraged in capital-intensive and technology-intensive industries.

(5) Special preferential tax policies for investments involving the introduction of advanced technology will be encouraged. Such

policies will permit the products of such enterprises to be sold on the domestic market, thus resolving their need for foreign exchange.

(6) The establishment of joint stock companies and the opening of new channels through which multinationals can make investments in China will be encouraged (already more than 20 joint stock companies involving foreign investments are listed on the Chinese stock market).

(7) Further development and improvement of the country's stock market will greatly boost the issue of B-shares of the large and medium-sized State-owned listed companies.

The readjustment of a series of economic administrative systems and policies will generally help improve the environment for foreign investment in China, bringing China's economic environment and domestic conditions in line with generally accepted international principles.

CONCLUSION

Before investing in China, investors are advised to carefully study the program of policies relating to the sector in which they intend to invest. China has developed a very elaborate legal system to provide protection for foreign investment. At the same time, the system is often subject to policy parameters which are established at the central government level. Therefore, when looking to invest in China, investors are advised to study carefully the policy directions currently in force and to seek the support of government officials and concerned ministries.

A list of the sectors where foreign investment is encouraged, restricted, or prohibited entirely appears in Appendix I.

CHAPTER 3

AN OVERVIEW OF THE RULES
AFFECTING FOREIGN INVESTORS

The development of China's legal system has been remarkable when compared to that of other countries. When China opened up its economic policy with the four modernisations in the early 1980s, there were only a few laws in effect, most focusing on domestic matters. Over a period of 15 years, China has put in place an entire and elaborate system of law for foreign investment covering a wide range of areas from investment vehicles to foreign exchange legislation to taxation, to trade and dispute resolution. China has also begun to promulgate legislation to govern the emergence of securities markets in Shenzhen and Shanghai. This legislation has already opened the door to the enormous potential of developing a securities industry in China. (See Chapter 16 for more information on securities markets.) To complement this legislation, a Companies Law covering outstanding issues relating to shareholding and bankruptcy was introduced in 1994.

This chapter outlines the basic structure of the legal system as it pertains to foreign investment and provides a number of practical tips on how this general system operates. The three major vehicles through which foreign investors may invest are described in later chapters. Chapter 4 covers Chinese–foreign equity joint ventures; Chinese–foreign cooperative joint ventures are described in Chapter 5; and Chapter 6 describes wholly foreign-owned enterprises. The three different types of enterprise are subject to the jurisdiction of special laws and regulations.

Under the Chinese legal system, new economic laws are adopted by the National People's Congress. These laws, while lacking specific details, state general principles and crystallise policy. Gaps in the law are meant to be filled later by 'implementing regulations', usually passed by the State Council, which qualify the law and state the implementation details.

There is often a time-lag of a year or more between the time a law is adopted by the National People's Congress and the implementation of regulations promulgated by the State Council. This system, although often criticised by foreign lawyers, works well because it gives the Government the necessary feedback to re-evaluate its economic reform and readjust the law to meet policy considerations and the needs of the people.

JOINT VENTURES

On 1 July 1979, the Fifth National People's Congress passed *The Law of the People's Republic of China on Chinese–Foreign Equity Joint Ventures* (the Joint Venture Law). This law established the basis for investing in China through the form of a joint venture, a structure modelled along the lines of a company, with a board of directors, a separate legal personality, and liability limited up to the contributions made by the parties to the joint venture.

On 20 September 1983, the State Council implemented Regulations for the Implementation of the Joint Venture Law. These regulations provided procedural details for establishing joint ventures, contributing capital, transferring technology, and the operations of the board of directors.

China's willingness to improve continuously on its legislation is demonstrated by the fact that on 4 April 1990, the Seventh National People's Congress revised the Joint Venture Law. The revised Law allows the foreign party to a joint venture to appoint the chairman of the board of directors (disallowed under the 1979 Joint Venture Law), and permits multiple parties to be participants in a joint venture (formerly restricted to one foreign and one Chinese party). The Joint Venture Implementing Regulations were shortly thereafter amended to allow joint ventures to be extended for periods of up to 50 years (formerly restricted to 20), and further amendments are being made. A new set of implementing regulations applying to cooperative joint ventures was adopted in 1996.

In the years following the adoption of the Joint Venture Law, many contractual joint ventures were established along the structure of a partnership. In the absence of any specific law, these enterprises followed loosely the concepts laid out in the Joint Venture Law. To address the question of this gap in the legislation, on 13 April 1988, the Seventh National People's Congress passed the law on Chinese–foreign cooperative joint ventures.

INVESTMENT VEHICLES

The Form of Investment You Choose is a Function of Balancing Management Control with Financial Exposure

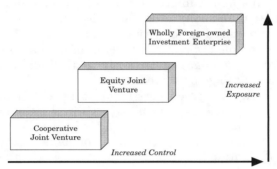

	Cooperative Joint Venture	Equity Joint Venture	Wholly Foreign-owned Investment Enterprise
STATUS	• Partner structure • May acquire status of legal entity if requirements are met and stated in contract	• Corporate structure • Status of legal entity	• Corporate structure • Status of legal entity
LIABILITY	• Individual liability of parties may be limited by parties in their contract	• Limited liability within limits of parties' capital	• Liability limited to registered capital
MANAGEMENT	• If registered as a legal entity board of directors must be established at the outset • If not established as a legal entity, a joint management committee should be set up	• Board of directors • Regulated by articles of association • Joint management and operation	• Board of directors • Regulated by articles of association • Autonomy in operation and management
CAPITAL CONTRIBUTION	• Law does not provide for capital contribution ratio between parties • Foreign: usually equipment and technology • Chinese: usually labour, land and cash	• Specific minimum on foreign party's contribution: 25% of registered capital • Foreign: usually equipment and technology • Chinese: usually labour, land and cash • Set time schedule for putting up contribution	• Solely from foreign investors
RESTRICTIONS	• Nil	• Nil	• Advanced technology • Export oriented
PROFIT-SHARING	• According to ratio specified in contract	• According to capital contribution ratio	• No sharing, entirely for the foreign pocket
TERMINATION	• According to the contract	• Terms: generally 10–50 years	• No perpetual succession

17

FOREIGN-OWNED ENTERPRISES

The National People's Congress adopted the law on wholly foreign-owned investment enterprises in 1986. This law permitted wholly foreign-owned enterprises to be established within the People's Republic of China, and made the Chinese legal system in this regard far more liberal than many other jurisdictions in Asia. While local participation is required in countries such as Malaysia and Thailand, China permits complete foreign ownership of a legal entity, provided that such entity is engaged in activities which involve either technology transfer or export production.

To further clarify the procedures involved in establishing a foreign investment enterprise in China, the Chinese Government has implemented a number of regulations addressing such issues as the management of labour, the registration of joint ventures and the contribution of capital.

FOREIGN EXCHANGE CONTROLS

China's own currency, the Renminbi, is a domestic currency and, at the time of writing (1996), is not freely convertible. Therefore, China's system of foreign exchange control prevents foreign investors from remitting their profits abroad, unless these profits already exist in the form of foreign exchange.

In December 1980, the State Council promulgated the Provisional Regulations for Foreign Exchange Control, which gave the State Administration of Exchange Control, under the People's Bank of China, supervisory and approval authority over foreign exchange transactions. Between 1981 and 1985, the State Administration of Exchange Control introduced a series of rules for implementing these Provisional Regulations. These rules governed foreign exchange held by individuals, foreign representatives in China and foreign investment enterprises, and also governed the transfer of precious metals. The rules also spelt out the penalties for violations.

As these controls were found to be burdensome and discouraging to foreign investors, China reacted by promulgating Regulations concerning the Balance of Foreign Exchange in Income and Expenditures by Joint Ventures (the Balancing Regulations) on 15 January 1986. These basically allowed joint ventures to utilise their Renminbi earnings in such a way as to generate foreign exchange income. Methods permitted under these regulations included using Renminbi to purchase domestic goods for export, import substitution, swapping Renminbi and foreign exchange between related joint ventures, pricing for foreign exchange to limited markets, and reinvesting Renminbi in China.

Between 1986 and 1989, the State Planning Commission, State Council, and State Administration of Exchange Control, as well as the Ministry of Foreign Economic Relations and Trade, promulgated additional measures to implement particular sections of the Balancing Regulations, which later led to the opening of foreign exchange Swap Centres. These Swap Centres are now being dismantled and replaced by the China Foreign Exchange Trading System, which is an interbank market based in Shanghai with branches throughout the country. Foreign exchange is discussed more fully in Chapter 15.

INTELLECTUAL PROPERTY

In 1983, the National People's Congress adopted *The Trademark Law of the People's Republic of China.* This law is fully discussed in Chapter 18. The Trademark Law is a modern piece of legislation drawn from extensive research carried out by Chinese specialists who worked in Japan, the United States and a number of European countries as well as with the World Intellectual Property Organisation of the United Nations. The Trademark Law led to the following major developments:

- the emergence of the concept of exclusive rights in China;
- the introduction of a voluntary registration system;
- clear procedures for trademark application examination and registration;
- the linking of trademark rights to quality control; and
- China's entry into membership of the Paris Convention for the Protection of Intellectual Property.

The Patent Law of the People's Republic of China was introduced in 1985. This provided protection for both domestic and foreign inventions and sparked off an invention boom in China. Following its introduction, a number of Chinese patent agents were established in Beijing, Shanghai and Hong Kong. The Patent Law was almost immediately followed by Detailed Rules and Regulations for Implementing the Patent Law promulgated by the State Council. To satisfy foreign investor concerns over the protection of computer software, specific regulations were promulgated by the Government to protect computer software and to establish a system of registration.

Chapter 19 has more information on the Patent Law, and Chapter 20 deals with copyright issues.

As a result of these developments, China's system for the protection of intellectual property is complete. The only drawback is the size of the country, which leads to difficulties in administering and carrying out anti-infringement action. However, as more qualified personnel are trained, administration should become easier.

SPECIAL ECONOMIC ZONES

The Special Economic Zones (SEZs) of China are established in Shenzhen, Zhuhai, Xiamen and San Tou and on Hainan Island. Throughout the 1980s, these were zones for experimentation with economic reform and for new legislation to cope with foreign investment and new concentrations of capital within Chinese society. Each of the zones has introduced its own legislation to govern investment, as well as approval procedures relating to foreign investment enterprises. Often before national legislation is passed at the Chinese Government level, an SEZ will promulgate its own legislation to test its effectiveness.

In addition, many major cities have established economic and technology zones which, like the SEZs, offer special tax preferences and other incentives. Each of these zones has local legislation governing its economic activities and investments.

ARBITRATION PRACTICES

As part of an effort to bring China's arbitration practice up to international standards, the China Council for the Promotion of International Trade (CCPIT) adopted a set of new rules on 12 September 1988. Under the new rules, the China International Economic and Trade Arbitration Commission (CIETAC) settles disputes arising from trade transactions. On 31 August 1994, the Standing Committee of the National People's Congress adopted a new law—*The Arbitration Law of The People's Republic of China* (the Arbitration Law)—to deal with arbitration issues in connection with contract disputes and property rights disputes in China.

The Arbitration Law has eight chapters which, for the first time, specifically and systematically address issues such as the organisation of arbitration tribunals, arbitration agreements, arbitration procedures, application of revocation of arbitral decisions and execution of the arbitral judgment. There is a special chapter (Chapter 8) wholly devoted to foreign arbitration issues. A foreign arbitration committee may be established by CIETAC, which may also stipulate the arbitration rules in accordance with the relevant provisions of the Arbitration Law and the Civil Procedure Law of the PRC.

The functions of CIETAC are to:

- operate independently and impartially;
- preside over arbitration cases; and
- decide on the validity of arbitration agreements.

CIETAC, located in Beijing, may establish sub-commissions in other cities in China in accordance with arbitration needs. On 1 June 1994, CIETAC adopted arbitration rules which all who practice arbitration have to follow. In the event of an arbitration case arising, CIETAC will select and appoint a panel of arbitrators which may include Chinese as well as foreigners. The disputing parties to an arbitration case may authorise attorneys to submit to CIETAC matters related to the dispute. The attorneys may be citizens of China or of foreign countries. When acting on behalf of a party, the attorney must produce a power of attorney to CIETAC.

CIETAC is also empowered to freeze the assets of a defendant by making an application to the local Chinese court where the defendant's properties are located, or where the arbitration is taking place. Each side may either appoint arbitrators from the panel of arbitrators, or authorise the chairman of CIETAC to make the appointments. Afterwards, the chairman will be appointed the third arbitrator to preside over the tribunal.

If both parties agree to appoint a sole arbitrator as the arbitration tribunal, they must reach a consensus on the appointment within 20 days of the application for arbitration, otherwise the chairman of CIETAC makes the appointment himself. If the appointed arbitrator has an interest in the case, he may request to be withdrawn from the tribunal.

The rules go on to state that arbitration may be carried out either through court hearings or, if both parties agree, it may be carried out outside the courts through examination of the written documents involved in the case. If both parties so require, an open trial may be held at the discretion of the arbitration tribunal. According to the rules, cases may be conducted where the arbitration commission is located, or at other locations upon the approval of the chairman of CIETAC.

Arbitration awards shall be final. Neither party may appeal to the courts or request other institutions to alter the arbitral awards. Although Chinese is the official language of CIETAC, translators may be provided. (For more information, see Chapter 13.)

GUAN XI

China's traditional political system was fundamentally a pattern of personal relationships. Today, personal relationships known as *guan xi* form an invisible network which often provides the most expedient way of getting anything done (from buying a train ticket to seeking official approval in establishing an enterprise). Therefore, the extent of one's own personal *guan xi* may determine the legality of what one does. Using one's *guan xi* to understand the informal systems beneath the law may also help one second-guess policy.

Given the recent proliferation of Chinese legislation, it is easy to assume that the written law in itself is the law. Unaware of the informal systems functioning beyond the statute, a foreigner may find himself working with only part of the system.

CONCLUSION

Despite China's enormous strides in introducing new legislation, China's legal system continues to develop within the context of a planned economy and central bureaucracy. Internal politics, policy considerations and traditional influences are often dominant factors operating behind the law. In many respects, the practical application of law in China actually begins not with the written law but with a complex network of informal systems operating beneath the formal legal one. These informal systems, although social in nature, play an implicit, pervasive role in the way law functions in China.

While *guan xi* and connections still play a very important part in doing business in China, the once widespread and broad decision-making powers of officials have to a great extent been curtailed and reframed into procedural decision-making within the scope of the legal system.

We are also seeing the rise of the National People's Congress—in the past often criticised by Western observers as being a 'rubber stamp' of party policy—which is maturing and exerting its powers as the nation's highest legislative authority.

PART 2
FORMS OF INVESTMENT

CHINESE–FOREIGN EQUITY JOINT VENTURES

The Law of the People's Republic of China on Chinese–Foreign Equity Joint Ventures (the Joint Venture Law) is the basic law on establishing Chinese–foreign equity joint ventures. The Joint Venture Law was promulgated and came into effect at the Second Session of the Fifth National People's Congress on 1 July 1979, and served as China's first law on accepting direct foreign investment since the policy of opening to the outside world was adopted. Regulations for the implementation of the Joint Venture Law were promulgated by the State Council and came into effect on 20 September 1983. These regulations addressed various problems involved in establishing Chinese–foreign equity joint ventures.

The Joint Venture Law was amended and revised at the Third Session of the Seventh National People's Congress in April 1990. In the revision, China took into account the concerns of foreign investors. The main contents of this legislation are discussed in the following pages.

The Joint Venture Law stipulates that an equity joint venture established within the territory of China must be approved by the Chinese Government and registered accordingly. Joint ventures in China are legal entities and subject to the jurisdiction and protection of Chinese Law. An equity joint venture takes the form of a limited liability company. The liability of each party (investor) to a joint venture is limited to the capital subscribed by it. Parties to an equity joint venture are jointly responsible for investment and management, and share risks, gains and losses. All assets are liable in the payment of debts.

PARTIES TO AN EQUITY JOINT VENTURE

According to Joint Venture Law, the foreign joint venturers may be companies, enterprises, or other economic organisations formed under the laws of a foreign country and registered as a legal entity. The foreign joint venturers may also be individuals.

The Chinese joint venturers may be Chinese companies, enterprises or other economic organisations, namely, State-owned enterprises, collective enterprises, private enterprises and other economic organisations formed under the law of China, approved by the department in charge and registered as a legal entity. No party political or government body and no Chinese individuals can act as the Chinese joint venturer. The management of joint ventures is addressed in Chapter 8.

BASIC POLICY REQUIREMENTS

As a matter of general policy, joint ventures established within China's territory must promote the development of China's economy through the raising of scientific and technological levels. Joint ventures under application for establishment should, in accordance with government policy, comply with at least one of the following requirements:

(1) they must use advanced technical equipment and scientific managerial methods which help increase the variety, improve the quality and raise the output of products, and save energy and materials;

(2) they must be open to technical innovation so as to bring about quicker returns and bigger profits with less investment;

(3) they must help expand exports and thereby increase foreign currency receipts; and

(4) they must help train technical and managerial personnel.

However, the law also stipulates that an application for establishing a joint venture will not be approved if it is considered that it will:

• be detrimental to China's sovereignty;

• violate Chinese law;

• not conform with the requirements for the development of China's national economy;

• cause environmental pollution; and

• due to obvious inequity in the agreements, contracts and articles of association signed, impair the rights and interests of one of the parties.

MAIN INDUSTRIES OR FIELDS OF INVESTMENT

The Regulations for the Implementation of the Joint Venture Law stipulate that joint ventures must raise scientific and technological levels for the benefit of socialist modernisation. Joint ventures are mainly approved in the following industries:

- energy development, materials supply for buildings, chemical and metallurgical industries;
- machine manufacturing, instrument and meter industries and offshore oil exploitation equipment manufacturing;
- electronics and computer industries, and communication equipment manufacturing;
- light industrial, textile, foodstuffs, medicine, medical apparatus and packaging industries;
- agriculture and animal husbandry; and
- tourism and service trades (not including commercial enterprises).

The above-mentioned industries were listed in the 1983 regulations. Since then, the types of industries permitted have been extended and increased constantly. Appendix I gives more complete information. For example, they now include transport (including air, railway and highway transport), construction of power stations and exploiting of natural resources. Joint ventures are now permitted in most industries, except those restricted due to strategic or economic reasons. Likewise, at first only six regions (Beijing, Shanghai, Tianjin, Guangzhou, Qingdao, Dalian) were open to foreign investment in the early 1980s. Now virtually the entire country has been opened except for certain restricted regions.

APPROVAL PROCEDURES

The Regulations for the Implementation of the Joint Venture Law stipulate that the establishment of a joint venture in China is subject to examination and approval by the Ministry of Foreign Trade and Economic Cooperation (MOFTEC). Upon approval of a joint venture, MOFTEC issues an Approval Certificate. Alternatively, the people's governments in the concerned provinces, autonomous regions and municipalities directly under the Central Government, or relevant ministries or bureaus under the State Council, (referred to as 'the entrusted office') may be entrusted with the power to examine and approve the establishment of joint ventures that comply with the following conditions.

(1) The total amount of investment is within the limit set by the State Council and the source of capital of the Chinese ventures has been ascertained.

(2) No additional allocation of raw materials by the State is required and the national reserves of fuel, power and transportation, and foreign trade export quotas are not affected.

The entrusted office, after approving the establishment of a joint venture, notifies MOFTEC for the record, and MOFTEC issues the Approval Certificate directly.

The Joint Venture Law and its regulations stipulate that the following procedures be undertaken in seeking approval of a joint venture.

(1) It is the Chinese partner who submits to MOFTEC or the entrusted office:

- a project proposal, and
- a preliminary feasibility study on the joint venture to be established with a foreign partner.

(2) The parties to the venture must then conduct work centred around the feasibility study, and then proceed to negotiate and sign the joint venture contract and articles of association.

(3) When applying for the establishment of a joint venture, the Chinese partner is responsible for the submission of the following documents to the examining and approving authorities:

- a written application for the establishment of the joint venture;
- the feasibility study jointly prepared by the parties to the venture;
- the joint venture contract and the articles of association signed by representatives authorised by the parties to the venture;
- a list of candidates for chairman, vice-chairman and directors nominated by the parties to the venture; and
- written opinions concerning the establishment of the venture by the department in charge and the people's government of the province, autonomous region or municipality directly under the Central Government where the joint venture is located.

According to the needs of management, a joint venture may establish its branches and sales organisation domestically and overseas. If establishing branches overseas, the approval of MOFTEC is required: branches must be established in accordance with the law of the countries (areas) where they are located.

REGISTRATION

The Joint Venture Law states that the registering body for joint ventures is the State Administration for Industry and Commerce or any of its local and regional bureaus. Joint ventures must register within thirty (30) days of receiving the approval certificate. This is in accordance with the provisions of the Measures of the People's Republic of China for the Administration of the Registration of Chinese–Foreign Equity Joint Ventures.

Application for Registration

In applying for registration, a joint venture must submit the following documents and materials to the Administration for Industry and Commerce:

(1) a written application for registration signed and issued by the chairman of the board of directors;

(2) an approval certificate from the Chinese government;

(3) the contract and articles of association;

(4) the feasibility study;

(5) the legal certificate of commencement of business issued by the country (area) of the foreign joint venturer; and

(6) the approval documents for construction which are issued by the People's Government of the town and county where the joint venture is located. These approvals cover:

- environmental protection;
- building approvals; and
- provision of water and electricity.

The Administration for Industry and Commerce approves or disapproves the registration within one month of receipt of the above-mentioned documents. When approved, a business licence is issued and joint venture operations can commence on the same day.

Changes in Registration

If a joint venture desires to move to a new site, shift its production, increase or cut or transfer the registered capital, or extend the contract period, it must, with the approval documents, register the changes with the Administration for Industry and Commerce where the joint venture is located. In cases where the chairman of the board of directors or the general manager change, the joint venture must immediately register the changes and the business licence is amended.

REGISTERED CAPITAL AND INVESTMENT CONTRIBUTION

The registered capital of a joint venture refers to the investment amount actually registered at the Administration for Industry and Commerce for the establishment of the joint venture. It represents the total amount of actual investment subscribed by the parties to the joint venture, and does not include either third party or shareholder loans, or other forms of external financing.

The Joint Venture Law stipulates that the proportion of the foreign joint venturer's investment in an equity joint venture must be not less than 25% of its registered capital. No law stipulates the highest limit, and it may be more than 50% but certainly not 100%. A joint venture cannot reduce its registered capital during its term of operation. A joint venture or one party to it, however, may assign its investment subscribed. Any increase, assignment or other disposal of the registered capital of a joint venture should be approved at a meeting of the board of directors and submitted to the authorities for approval. Registration procedures for changes should be handled at the original registration administration office.

Each joint venturer may invest in cash or may contribute buildings, factory premises, equipment or other materials, industrial property, proprietary technology, or the right to the use of a site, appraised at appropriate value, as its investment. After the investment is paid by the parties to the joint venture, a Chinese registered accountant must verify it and provide a certificate of verification. The joint venture then issues investment certificates to the parties.

RELEVANT TAXES AND RATES

Although they vary according to type of business, taxes applicable to Chinese–foreign equity joint ventures are as follows:

Value Added Tax (VAT)

The basic rate is 17% but, in some cases, a lower rate may be applied; the lower rate is 13%. The lower rate applies to essential foodstuffs and agricultural production materials, etc.

Consumption Tax

Consumption tax is imposed on 11 items: tobacco, alcohol, cosmetics, skin-care and hair-care products, precious jewellery and precious jade and stones, firecrackers, gasoline, diesel oil, motor vehicle tyres, motorcycles and motor cars.

Either the amount-on-volume method or a fixed rate based on the sales price is the method of assessment. In the fixed rate method, consumption tax is calculated on the basis of the sales price including consumption tax but excluding VAT.

Business Tax

Business tax is imposed on the provision of taxable services, the transfer of intangible property and sales of immovable property: 3% is levied on transportation, communication, culture and sports; 5% on finance and insurance, the provision of taxable services, transfer of intangible property and sales of immovable property. For entertainment, the tax rates range from 5% to 20%.

Land Appreciation Tax

This tax is only levied on Chinese–foreign equity joint ventures that are engaged in the development of real estate. A progressive tax rate is applied:

- for that part of the appreciation amount not exceeding 50% of the sum of deductible items, the tax rate is 30%;
- for that part of the appreciation amount exceeding 50%, but not exceeding 100%, of the sum of deductible items, the tax rate is 40%;
- for that part of the appreciation amount exceeding 100%, but not exceeding 200%, of the sum of deductible items, the tax rate is 50%; and
- for that part of the appreciation amount exceeding 200% of the sum of deductible items, the tax rate is 60%.

Other Taxes

- *City Maintenance and Construction Tax*: the rate is 0.6% in urban districts, 0.4% in the country and in rural villages, and 0.2% elsewhere.

- *Urban Real Estate Tax*: a rate of 1.2%.
- *Enterprise Income Tax*: a rate of 30% and additional 3% for local tax, i.e., 33% in total.
- *Vehicles and Vessels Tax*: the rate differs according to the vehicle/vessel involved and number of seats. Generally it is very small.

DURATION OF A JOINT VENTURE

In accordance with the amended Joint Venture Law, if a joint venture undertakes projects encouraged by the authorities, the parties to it may or may not specify its duration in the contract. If the duration is not specified, then the termination conditions should be stated. The duration of the joint venture begins from the date when it is issued a business licence.

If a joint venture operates in the following areas, its duration should be specified in the contract.

(1) Service industries including hotels, apartments, office buildings, entertainment, catering trade, taxis, colour-enlarging and photo developing, maintenance, consultancy, beauty salons, etc.

(2) Real estatement development and management.

(3) Exploration and development of resources.

(4) Projects where the period of investment is limited by the State.

When all parties agree to extend the duration of a joint venture, they must file an application for extension with the examining and approving authorities six months before the expiry date. The authorities give an official written reply to the applicant within one month from the date of receipt of the application. Upon approval of the extension, the joint venture must undertake registration formalities for the alteration in accordance with the Measures for the Registration Administration mentioned earlier.

SETTLEMENT OF DISPUTES

Disputes arising over the interpretation or execution of the agreement, contract or articles of association must, if possible, be settled through friendly consultation or mediation. If these prove futile, the disputes become subject to arbitration or judicial settlement.

Parties to a joint venture must apply for arbitration in accordance with the relevant written agreement between them. They may submit the disputes to the Foreign Economic and Trade Arbitration Commission of the China Council for the Promotion of International Trade in accordance with its arbitration rules. With the consent of the parties concerned, arbitration can also be carried out by an arbitration agency in the country where the respondent is located or by one in a third country in accordance with the arbitration agency's rules.

In the absence of a written agreement on arbitration among the parties to a joint venture, any of the parties may bring a suit in a Chinese people's court. Chapter 13 contains further information on arbitration.

CONCLUSION

With the revision of the Joint Venture Law, China's corporate structure for foreign investments became further refined. In the future, there is likely to be no differentiation between domestic and foreign investment enterprises in China. At such time, the existing foreign investment legislation for equity joint ventures, cooperative joint ventures and wholly foreign-owned investment enterprises may merge into a single foreign investment law. Clearly it is China's intention to create a balanced situation between foreign and domestic enterprises to eliminate unnecessary privileges for either and to develop a system which is international in all respects.

CHAPTER 5

CHINESE–FOREIGN COOPERATIVE JOINT VENTURES

The Law of the People's Republic of China on Chinese–Foreign Cooperative Joint Ventures (the Law on Cooperative Joint Ventures) was adopted on 13 April 1988 at the First Session of the Seventh National People's Congress and came into force on the same day. A Chinese–foreign cooperative joint venture can generally be equated with a partnership. It is also referred to as a contractual joint venture, where the Chinese and foreign investors reach an agreement, in the cooperative joint venture contract, on such matters as:

- the conditions for investment or cooperation;
- the distribution of earnings or products;
- the sharing of risks and losses;
- the methods of operation and management; and
- the ownership of the assets at the termination of the joint venture.

Some people regard it as the primary stage in the development of the Chinese–foreign equity joint venture.

CHARACTERISTICS OF A COOPERATIVE JOINT VENTURE

The forms of cooperative operation are relatively flexible—the project can be large or small, the cooperative period can be long or short, and the amount of investments can be large or small. It is easy to reach an agreement and results of the investments can be seen over a shorter period. Cooperative operations are suitable for industries which do not require much technology. Since a cooperative joint venture is a contractual cooperative relationship based on the mutual confidence and knowledge of the parties, the parties to it can reach mutually satisfactory arrangements. For instance, one of the parties provides assets such as the building and the right of the use of land, while the other party provides capital and equipment to jointly achieve some specific project. The cooperative joint venture form is mainly applied to medium-size or small projects in the fields of housing, the construction of travel facilities, car renting, light manufacturing and processing industry, and so on. The duration of the cooperation and the form of profit distribution are stipulated in the contract.

The Chinese and foreign partners may wish to register the cooperative joint venture as a Chinese legal entity. If they do so, it must qualify as a legal entity as stipulated in the General Principles of Civil Law of the People's Republic of China. This states that:

- it must be established in accordance with law;
- it must have the necessary property or funds;
- it must have its own name, organisational structure and premises; and
- it must be able to assume civil obligations independently.

PARTIES TO A COOPERATIVE JOINT VENTURE

The Chinese partner can only be an enterprise or other economic organisation. Chinese nationals cannot sign cooperative joint venture contracts with foreigners. The foreign partner may may be a legal entity, i.e., an enterprise or an economic organisation, or an individual. When companies, enterprises or other economic organisations, or individuals from Hong Kong, Macau and Taiwan go to the mainland to establish cooperative joint ventures with inland enterprises or economic organisations, their applications will be handled with reference to the Law on Cooperative Joint Ventures.

FINANCIAL ARRANGEMENTS

A cooperative joint venture registered as a legal entity is a limited liability company and it assumes liability for debt within all its properties. Each party is liable to the cooperative joint venture to the extent of the capital subscribed or according to the conditions to which it contracted.

The total amount of investments of a cooperative joint venture registered a legal entity is the capital construction fund, or the technology transformation capital needed for the joint venture's production and scale of operations as stipulated in the contract and articles of association. In layman's terms, this is the sum of the registered capital and loans of the joint venture.

In a cooperative joint venture registered as a legal entity, the proportion of investments contributed by the foreign partner is not less then 25% of the registered capital. A cooperative joint venture not registered as a legal entity is one where the parties jointly provide capital and conditions, and operate in accordance with the provisions in the contract. It is an economic unity not registered as a legal entity.

Methods of Investment

The parties to a cooperative joint venture invest or provide conditions for cooperation as agreed upon in the contract. The investment contributed by the parties can be in cash, personal property, real estate or other property rights, and conditions necessary for the operation of the enterprise can be provided by the parties in the form of real estate and other property rights. The investments contributed by the parties which are not in the form of cash may be provided in the form of ownership (the right to the use of land, industrial property rights and non-patent technology). Such rights should be expressed in currency value. The parties invest with their own property and the investments do not have any form of real right for security.

Loans and Guarantees

The cooperative parties are jointly liable for the debts of a cooperative joint venture and must present guarantees from a bank or their parent company that they will fulfil their joint obligations.

The parties to a cooperative joint venture not registered as a legal entity can reach an agreement in the contract that at least one party can assume unlimited liabilities for the debt of the venture, and the other party is liable for debt within the limit of the capital subscribed or the conditions to which it contracted.

The party with unlimited liabilities has the right to represent the cooperative joint venture and is mainly responsible for the operation and management of the venture. He has the right to make final decisions when discussing major issues.

In a cooperative joint venture not registered as a legal entity, the proportion of investments contributed by the foreign partner must not be less than 25% of the total amount of contribution subscribed by the parties to the venture.

The cooperative conditions or investments provided by the parties to a cooperative joint venture not registered as a legal entity can be respectively or jointly possessed by the parties to the venture and managed and utilised by the venture. Neither party shall deal with the investments without authorisation.

Thus far most of the cooperative joint ventures established are cooperative joint ventures registered as a legal entity.

Profit-sharing

During the cooperation, the investments of the foreign investor are repaid in the form of:

- income-sharing distribution;
- product-sharing distribution; and
- profit-sharing distribution.

The investments of the Chinese and foreign partners are not based on an evaluation of the investment proportion and the dividends are not distributed in proportion to the amounts of investment but are agreed upon in the contract by the cooperative parties according to the specific situation. Often in the initial stage of the cooperation, the foreign partner will receive profit distribution relatively greater in order to repay his loans and investment. In the second stage of the cooperation, the distribution proportion of dividends between the Chinese and foreign partners may become equal. In the later stage, the distribution proportion of the Chinese partner may be higher than that of the foreign partner. Upon the expiration of the cooperation, the ownership of machinery and equipment invested by the foreign partner generally reverts to the Chinese partner because the income distribution during the cooperation period has taken into account the foreign partner's recovering his share of investments and profit.

Further Conditions

The time limit for investment or conditions for the cooperation are stipulated in the cooperative joint venture contract according to the construction period and the needs of the operation.

If the contract prescribes that the full investments be subscribed or all the conditions for cooperation be provided at one time, they must be subscribed or provided within 180 days from the date of issuance of the business licence or the registration certificate.

If the contract prescribes that the investments can be made and the conditions for cooperation be provided by instalment, the time limit for every instalment must be written in the contract. The first instalment should not be less than 15% of the full investments or conditions for cooperation and should be provided in full within a period of 90 days beginning from the day when the business licence or the registration certificate is issued. The time limit for the last instalment should not be later than two years from the day when the business licence or the registration certificate was issued.

If special circumstances require the postponement of a contribution, the approval of the original examining and approving authorities must be obtained.

If the partners fail to make contributions or provide the conditions for cooperation as stipulated in the contract without good reason, the examining and approving authorities have the right to rescind the approval certificate of the cooperative joint venture and notify the registration department to revoke the venture's business licence or registration certificate.

The investments made or conditions for cooperation provided by the parties should be verified by an accountant registered in China, who provides a verification report for submission to the original examining and approving authorities and registration authorities.

FIELDS OF INVESTMENT

A cooperative joint venture established within China's territory must be beneficial to the development of the national economy and to China's scientific and technological expertise. (Appendix I gives more complete information on this subject.) Economic benefits can also accrue to the parties to a cooperative joint venture. Generally, China encourages cooperative joint ventures in industries such as:

- energy;
- transportation;
- raw materials;
- electronics;
- machine manufacturing;
- agriculture;
- forestry;
- animal husbandry; and
- tourism and service trades.

The country especially encourages the establishment of export-oriented and technologically advanced enterprises. However, enterprises engaged in publishing, broadcasting, television, postal services and telecommunications are not permitted to establish cooperative joint ventures.

Application for the establishment of a cooperative joint venture will not be approved if it would involve any of the following situations:

- damage to China's sovereignty or to social and public interests;
- impairment of the country's national security;
- incompatibility with requirements for China's national economic development;
- possible creation of environmental pollution; and
- obviously unfair clauses in the signed contract that are injurious to the interests of one or several parties to the cooperative joint venture.

APPROVAL PROCEDURES

The establishment of a cooperative joint venture must be approved by the Ministry of Foreign Trade and Economic Cooperation (MOFTEC). As stipulated by the State Council, if the total amount of investment is within the power of the examining and approving authorities, the joint venture can be examined and approved by the Economic and Trade Administration Department of the province, autonomous region, municipality under the Central Government, Special Economic Zone separately listed on the State plan, and the coastal economic development zone where the joint venture is established.

If the Chinese partners are economic organisations subsidiary to the ministry, committee and bureau of the State Council, the joint venture must be examined and approved by those bodies. If the total amount of the project investment exceeds the powers of the examining and approving authorities, or the country has to consider its impact on fuel, power, communications and transportation, the joint venture must be approved by MOFTEC.

Submission of Documents

The Chinese partner is responsible for the submission of the following documents to the examining and approving authorities:

- a written application for the establishment of the cooperative joint venture and its approval documents;
- the feasibility study jointly prepared by the parties to the cooperative joint venture;
- the cooperative joint venture contract and articles of association signed by the representatives authorised by the parties;

- the business licence or the registration certificate of the investors, the yearly statements of assets and liabilities for the last three years or other credit position certifying documents;
- a list of candidates for chairman, vice-chairman and directors of the joint venture which is about to be established, or the director, deputy director and members of the joint managerial committee; and
- other documents thought necessary by the examining and approving authorities.

All the documents except the credit position certifying documents must be written in Chinese. The feasibility study, contract, articles of association and list of candidates for the board of directors may be written simultaneously in a foreign language agreed upon by the parties to the venture. Where the two versions come into conflict with each other, the Chinese version will prevail.

Approval Certificate

The examination and approval authorities examine the contract, articles of association and other documents submitted to them and decide whether or not to approve them within 45 days. A cooperative joint venture approved by the ministry, committee and bureau of the State Council is issued the approval certificate by MOFTEC; the contract and articles of association come into force on the date the approval certificate is issued.

Registration

The Chinese partner must within 30 days of the receipt of the approval certificate register with the State Administration for Industry and Commerce where the cooperative joint venture is located. The registration authorities will issue a business licence to a cooperative joint venture registered as a legal entity and a business registration certificate to a cooperative joint venture not registered as a legal entity within 30 days of the receipt of all the application documents.

The date of issue of the business licence or the registration certificate is the date of the establishment of a cooperative joint venture. A cooperative joint venture must within 30 days of its establishment carry out tax registration with the tax authorities.

ORGANISATION, STRUCTURE AND MANAGEMENT

A cooperative joint venture registered as a legal entity must establish a board of directors. The board of directors is the highest authority of the venture and can decide all the major issues concerning it. The chairman and vice-chairman of the board are appointed through consultation by the parties to the venture or are elected by the board. The following issues must be unanimously agreed upon by the board of directors:

- any amendment to the articles of association of the venture;
- any changes to or assignment of the registered capital or changes in the conditions for cooperation;
- the formulation of and amendment to the important rules and regulations of the venture;
- the mortgage of the assets; and
- the termination of the venture before the due date or its merger with another economic organisation.

The board of directors must establish a management office which is responsible for the day-to-day management and operations. The management office has a general manager and one or several deputy general mangers. The general manager, deputy general managers and other high-ranking managerial personnel are the employees of the cooperative joint venture and they must represent its interests. They must not favour either party to the venture or get involved in other economic organisations' commercial competition against their own enterprise.

A cooperative joint venture not registered as a legal entity must establish a joint managerial committee which consists of the representatives appointed by the parties to the venture. This committee will manage the joint venture on behalf of the two parties to the venture. The joint managerial committee can decide whether to establish the management organisation and will directly manage the cooperative joint venture if no such organisation is established.

Any dispute between the parties to a cooperative joint venture arising from the interpretation or execution of the contract must be settled through consultation or mediation. If the dispute cannot be settled through consultation or mediation, the parties can go to a Chinese arbitration agency or the arbitration agency of the defendant's country or any other arbitration agency in accordance with a written agreement. The Chinese or foreign party may bring a suit in a Chinese court if there is no arbitration clause between the parties to the venture. (Chapter 13 discusses arbitration more fully).

DISTRIBUTION OF EARNINGS AND RECOVERY OF INVESTMENT

The parties to a cooperative joint venture can distribute earnings by way of profit and product distribution or other distribution methods agreed upon by them. The specific form and proportion of earnings distribution must be stated in the cooperative joint venture contract. The amount of tax to be paid is calculated in accordance with the tax law.

If a cooperative joint venture contract prescribes that upon the expiration of the period of the venture's operation all the fixed assets belong to the Chinese partner without compensation, the foreign partner can recover his investment ahead of time. While the cooperative joint venture is still operating, he can:

- increase the distribution proportion of the foreign partner based on that agreed upon between himself and the Chinese partner in the contract;
- recover his investment prior to the payment of income tax if the financial and tax authorities approve; or
- initiate some other form of investment recovery approved by the financial and tax authorities.

The profit and other legitimate income in foreign exchange can be remitted abroad through a cooperative joint venture's bank account. Salaries and other legitimate earnings in foreign exchange can be remitted freely after payment of the tax according to the law.

DURATION OF A COOPERATIVE JOINT VENTURE

The duration of a cooperative joint venture is decided through consultation between the Chinese and foreign partners and must be clearly stipulated in the contract before the contract is submitted to the examining and approving authorities for approval. If the parties intend to extend the duration of the venture, they must file an application with the original examining and approving authorities 180 days before the expiration of the venture, stating the situation regarding an extension of contract, and the reasons for and purposes of the extension. The authorities will decide whether to approve within 30 days of receipt of the application.

If the cooperative joint venture contract prescribes that the foreign partner recover his investment ahead of time and the investment has been fully recovered, the duration of the venture will not be extended. If the foreign partner increases his investment, he can apply for an extension of the joint venture. If part of the foreign partner's investment has been recovered, the parties can decide the distribution proportion when distributing the remaining assets. The amount of assets distributed to the foreign partner who has recovered part of his investment cannot exceed the amount of investments which has not been recovered.

CONCLUSION

The cooperative joint venture structure is in many ways more flexible than that of the equity joint venture. Currently, equity joint ventures have very strict requirements, with the distribution of profits/liabilities strictly controlled according to the rate of equity defined in the contract. In the case of cooperative joint ventures, however, the distribution of profits may be flexible based on the contractual agreement decided between the two parties.

Because of this, many foreign investors prefer to establish a cooperative joint venture for projects involving real estate and manufacturing. Today, there are certainly far more cooperative joint ventures then equity joint ventures and, in the opinion of Chinese as well as foreign investors, approvals for the former are easier to obtain.

CHAPTER 6

WHOLLY FOREIGN–OWNED
INVESTMENT ENTERPRISES

A wholly foreign-owned investment enterprise is an independent legal entity entirely owned by the foreign investor. Such enterprises are usually permitted in sectors which involve either hi-tech transfer or the export of the major part of production. Nevertheless, in many regions more liberal approaches are being taken as wholly foreign-owned investment enterprises are being approved for a number of non-manufacturing sectors including consulting.

A wholly foreign-owned enterprise is one of the three vehicles through which China allows direct foreign investment. It is established in China by foreign investors, exclusively with their own capital, in accordance with relevant Chinese laws. It can register as a Chinese legal entity and independently perform production and operation activities, subject to the examination, approval and issue of the business licence.

The Law of the People's Republic of China on Wholly Foreign-owned Enterprises (the Law on Wholly Foreign-owned Enterprises) was adopted by the National People's Congress in April 1986. The law and its rules consist of not only the general principles for establishment, the legal status of the enterprise, the conditions for and scope of the establishment and the rules for encouraging and managing the enterprise, but also the procedures and principles for operating and managing it.

Firstly, the investments within China's territory by a foreign investor, the profits due him and his other legitimate rights and interests are protected by Chinese law. Article 5 of the Law on Wholly Foreign-owned Enterprises clearly stipulates that: 'The state shall not nationalise or requisition any wholly foreign-owned enterprise. Under special circumstances, when public interest requires, wholly foreign-owned enterprises may be requisitioned by following legal procedure and appropriate compensation shall be made.' Article 19 stipulates that: 'The foreign investor can remit abroad the lawful profits earned from a wholly foreign-owned enterprise, other lawful earnings and the remaining funds after liquidation. The wages, salaries and other legitimate income earned by the foreign employee from a wholly foreign-owned enterprise may be remitted abroad after the payment of individual income tax in accordance with the Law.' The law permits a wholly foreign-owned enterprise to make and implement a production and operation plan on its own. No person or administrative department can intervene with the decision-making power of a wholly foreign-owned enterprise.

Secondly, a wholly foreign-owned enterprise must abide by Chinese laws and regulations and must not engage in any activities detrimental to China's public interests. Article 3 of the Law on Wholly Foreign-owned Enterprises stipulates that: 'The establishment of a wholly foreign-owned enterprise must be beneficial to the development of China's national economy and shall advance technology and equipment, and all or almost all of the products are for exportation.'

CONDITIONS FOR ESTABLISHING A WHOLLY FOREIGN-OWNED ENTERPRISE

According to Article 1 of the Law on Wholly Foreign-owned Enterprises, a foreign investor may be a foreign enterprise or other economic organisation or individual. A wholly foreign-owned enterprise in China may be exclusively or jointly invested.

Article 3 of the Rules for the Implementation of the Law on Wholly Foreign-owned Enterprises stipulates that: 'The establishment of a wholly foreign-owned enterprise must be conducive to the development of China's national economy and capable of gaining remarkable economic results and shall meet at least one of the following conditions:

- use advanced technology and equipment, engage in the development of new products, conserve energy and raw materials, and realise the upgrading of products and the replacement of old products with new ones which can be used for replacing similar imported goods;
- its annual output value of export products accounts for more than 50% of the annual output value of all products, thereby realising the balance between revenues and expenditure in foreign exchange or with a surplus.'

Article 4 of the rules clearly prohibits wholly foreign-owned enterprises in the following trades:

- the press, publishing, broadcasting television, and movies;
- domestic commerce, foreign trade, and insurance; and
- postal services and telecommunications.

In addition, Article 5 of the rules places restrictions on foreign ownership in such areas as public utilities, communications and transportation, real estate, trust investment and leasing. An application for the establishment of a wholly foreign-owned enterprise in the above areas must be submitted to the Ministry of Foreign Trade and Economic Cooperation (MOFTEC) for approval, except as otherwise provided by Chinese laws and regulations.

FORMS OF CONTRIBUTING INVESTMENT

According to Article 26 of the Rules for the Implementation of the Law on Wholly Foreign-owned Enterprises, a foreign investor can make all or part of the contribution in cash. Cash refers to convertible foreign exchange or the Renminbi profits earned by the foreign investor from other wholly foreign-owned enterprises in China.

A foreign investor can contribute machinery and equipment, industrial property rights and proprietary technology as investment. Machinery and equipment must be:

(1) those needed for production by the enterprise; and

(2) those that cannot be produced in China, or that can be produced in China but cannot be guaranteed to meet requirements in terms of technical performance or supply date.

The value placed on the machinery and equipment must not be higher than the normal price for similar machinery and equipment sold on the international market at the time. The industrial property rights and proprietary technology, being assigned a certain value and used as contributing investment, must be:

(1) owned by the foreign investors themselves; and

(2) capable of producing new products that are urgently needed by China, or that are suitable for export and marketable abroad.

The assigning of a fixed value on the industrial property rights and proprietary technology must conform with the general evaluation principles of the international market; the value must not exceed 20% of the registered capital of the wholly foreign-owned enterprises.

ESTABLISHMENT PROCEDURES

A foreign investor must submit a report to the local people's government at or above the county level at the place where the proposed enterprise is to be established. The report should include the aim of the proposed enterprise; the scope and scale of business operation; the products to be produced; the technology and equipment to be adopted and used; the proportion of the sales of products between the domestic market and the foreign market; the area of land to be used and the related requirements; the conditions and quantities of water, electricity, coal, coal gas and other forms of energy resources required; and the requirement of public infrastructure.

The local people's government will, within 30 days of receiving the report, give a reply in writing to the foreign investor. The reply does not constitute an examination and approval of the project; it states whether the conditions required for the establishment of the proposed enterprise can be met. After obtaining a positive reply, the foreign investor must submit an application to the examination and approval authorities through the local people's government at or above the county level at the place where the enterprise is to be established.

Documents to be Submitted

The following documents must be submitted to the examination and approval authorities:

- the written application for the establishment of a wholly foreign-owned enterprise;
- a feasibility study;
- the articles of association of the enterprise;
- the name-list of the legal representatives (or the candidates for membership of the board of directors) of the enterprise;
- the legal 'certifying documents' and financial documents of the foreign investor;
- the written reply given by the people's government at or above the county level at the place where the enterprise is to be established; and
- an inventory of goods and materials for import.

The 'certifying documents' mentioned above primarily refer to:

- the documents certifying the foreign investor is a legal entity in his country or region of origin;
- the name-list of the board of directors;
- the documents certifying the qualifications of the legal representative;

- the statements of assets and liabilities over the past three years; and

- proof of nationality and status, personal details (in the form of a resume) and assets held by the foreign investor if the investment is made in the name of a private individual.

The examination and approval authorities may request the foreign investor to notarise the above certifying documents and materials in his country or region of origin.

If the foreign investor intends to use the machinery and equipment (having been assigned a fixed value) as his investment, a detailed inventory list including the names, categories, quantities and the values assigned to the machinery and equipment must be submitted to the examination and approval authorities as an appendix to the application for the establishment of the enterprise. Details of industrial property rights and proprietary technology (having been assigned a fixed value) including a duplicate of the proprietary rights certificate, the effective condition of the equipment, its standard of technological performance, its actual value and the basis and standard for the calculation of pricing, must be submitted to the examination and approval authorities as an appendix to the application.

In the event that two or more foreign investors jointly file an application for the establishment of a wholly foreign-owned enterprise, they must submit a duplicate of the contract.

Powers of the Examination and Approval Authorities

The level of authority required to examine and approve a wholly foreign-owned enterprise depends on the total amount of investment and the industry involved. Projects which are restricted according to Article 5 of the Rules for the Implementation of the Law on Wholly Foreign-owned Enterprises, must be examined and approved by MOFTEC. If the foreign investor applies for the establishment of another form of wholly foreign-owned enterprise (except in the form of limited liability), the local government of the province, city, autonomous region, municipality, or Special Economic Zone where the enterprise is located, examines and comments on the application before submitting it to MOFTEC for examination and approval. When the total amount of investment exceeds the authority of the local people's government, the application by the enterprise is examined and approved by MOFTEC.

If the total amount of investment is within the approval authority of the local people's government, and does not place a burden on the country's systems of communication and transportation, the supply of raw materials, fuel and electricity, the sale market, or the export quotas for foreign trade, then the local people's government can examine and approve the application.

The examination and approval authorities at all levels will, within 90 days of receiving all the required documents for the establishment of a wholly foreign-owned enterprise, make a decision whether to approve the application. In the event that the documents are not complete, or some are inappropriate, it may be necessary to make up the deficiency within a prescribed time limit. An approval certificate is issued after the application is examined and approved by the relevant authorities.

Registration

Following the approval of the application, the foreign investor must, within 30 days of receiving the certificate of approval, file an application for registration with the relevant administrative department for industry and commerce, and obtain a business licence. The date on which the business licence is issued is the date of the establishment of the enterprise. In the event that the foreign investor fails to file the application within 30 days of receiving the certificate of approval, the certificate becomes invalid automatically.

REGISTERED CAPITAL

A foreign investor in a wholly foreign-owned enterprise, which is in the form of a limited liability company, is liable for the debts of the enterprise up to the limit of the investment he has subscribed, i.e., the limit of the capital registered in the State Administration for Industry and Commerce.

A foreign investor may make the investment contribution in instalments. The first instalment must not be less than 15% of the total amount of registered capital the foreign investor has undertaken to make, and must be made in full within 90 days of the day when the business licence was issued. The last instalment must be made three years from the day when the business licence was issued.

After the foreign investor has paid the investment in full, the enterprise must engage a Chinese registered accountant to prepare a report to verify the amount of capital. This report must be submitted to the body that issued the approval and, for the record, to the State Administration for Industry and Commerce.

A wholly foreign-owned enterprise cannot reduce its registered capital during its term of operation. Any increase in or assignment of the registered capital of the enterprise is subject to approval by the approving body. The enterprise must go through the State Administration for Industry and Commerce if there are any changes in the registration details.

PURCHASING OF RAW MATERIALS AND MARKETING OF PRODUCTS

A wholly foreign-owned enterprise is entitled to make its own decisions on the purchase, for its own use, of machinery and equipment, raw and processed materials, fuels, parts and components, fittings, primary parts, means of transport and articles for office use. The enterprise may purchase either in China or from overseas, but if the terms are similar, priority must be given to purchase in China.

A wholly foreign-owned enterprise is entitled to sell its products on the Chinese or overseas markets in accordance with the approved sales proportion between the two markets. It may also appoint a Chinese commercial agency to sell its products on a commission basis.

Where machinery and equipment are assigned a fixed value and are used by a foreign investor as contributing investment, the investor must file an application directly, or through an agency, to obtain import licences. Where the import of materials and export of products involve the management of import and export licences, the enterprise must work out an annual plan for importation and exportation, and apply, every six months, to the license-issuing body for the licence.

The purchase and sale prices for importation and exportation are set with reference to the current price on the international market and are supervised by the tax authorities. The evasion of tax using such methods as importing at high prices while exporting at low prices is prohibited.

FINANCIAL ARRANGEMENTS

A wholly foreign-owned enterprise is an independent economic entity, and its financial affairs and accounting system must be supervised. Supervision rights are granted to the relevant authorities who monitor and encourage the enterprise to engage in orderly operation, and ensure that the enterprise pays taxes and various administrative expenses according to law.

Accounting System

Article 14 of the Law on Wholly Foreign-owned Enterprises stipulates that: 'A wholly foreign-owned enterprise must set up account books in China, conduct independent accounting, submit the fiscal reports and statements as required and accept supervision by the financial and tax authorities. If a wholly foreign-owned enterprise refuses to maintain account books in China, the financial and tax authorities may impose a fine on it, and the industry and commerce administration authorities may order it to suspend operations or may revoke its business licence. In order to assure the truthfulness of the accounting statement, the accounting statements of a wholly foreign-owned enterprise and its liquidation may be valid only after verification by a Chinese registered accountant, who will also prepare a certificate.'

Reserve Funds

Reserve funds and bonus and welfare funds for workers and staff members are taken out of profits after a wholly foreign-owned enterprise has paid income tax in accordance with the provisions of the Chinese tax law. The proportion of reserve funds to be withdrawn must not be lower than 10% of the total amount of profits after tax. The withdrawal of reserve funds may be stopped when the total cumulative reserve has reached 50% of the registered capital. The proportion of bonus and welfare funds for workers and staff members to be withdrawn is determined by the enterprise.

Foreign Exchange Balance

Achieving a balance in foreign exchange is a basic requirement to safeguard the operation and development of a wholly foreign-owned enterprise. Both the Law on Wholly Foreign-owned Enterprises and its rules for implementation emphasise: 'A Wholly Foreign-owned Enterprise shall achieve by itself the balance of revenues and expenditures in foreign exchange.' The enterprise must achieve nationally the sales proportion between the domestic and the foreign market and increase its foreign exchange-earning capacity to pay the legitimate profits of the investors and the salaries and wages of foreign personnel.

Besides the above general provisions, the Law on Wholly Foreign-owned Enterprises and its rules for implementation also have relatively flexible provisions on the balance in foreign exchange. If an enterprise adopts advanced technology, machinery and equipment to produce goods which replace similar imported goods, and is permitted to sell the products in China, and then consequently experiences an imbalance in foreign exchange, the relevant authorities will help them correct the imbalance.

Taxation

A wholly foreign-owned enterprise must, within 30 days of its establishment, register with the tax authorities. The following goods and materials imported by the enterprise are exempt from customs duties and consolidated industrial and commercial taxes:

(1) the machinery and equipment, parts and components, building and other materials used as investment by the foreign investor and needed for construction, as well as the installation and reinforcement of machinery;

(2) the machinery and equipment, parts and components, means of communication and transportation for use in production and equipment for use in production and management, imported, for its own use, by the enterprise with the funds included in the total amount of investment; and

(3) the raw materials and processed materials, auxiliary materials, primary parts, parts and components, and articles and materials for packaging imported by the enterprise for the production of export products.

In the event that the imported goods and materials are resold within China, or are used in the production of products to be sold within the territory of China, the enterprise concerned must pay the taxes or make up the taxes in accordance with the provisions of the tax law of China. The export commodities produced by the enterprise, except those whose exportation is restricted by China, are exempt from customs duties and consolidated industrial and commercial taxes.

A wholly foreign-owned enterprise must pay taxes and duties in accordance with the provisions of Chinese laws. The income tax rate on such an enterprise in the Special Economic Zones and the economic and technological development zones of the coastal opening cities is 15%; the income tax rate on a wholly foreign-owned enterprise in other regions is 30%. In addition, the 'export-oriented' and 'technologically advanced' enterprises may enjoy favourable treatment such as exemption from income tax of the remitting profits and reduction in income tax. Article 17 of the Law on Wholly Foreign-owned Enterprises stipulates that: 'An enterprise that reinvests its profits in China after paying income tax, and which has been in business no less than five years, may apply for refund of a part of the income tax already paid on the reinvested amount.'

A wholly foreign-owned enterprise is administered in accordance with law and supervised by the administrative departments of the PRC on matters of foreign exchange, customs, accounting, auditing, taxation, and industry and commerce.

LABOUR MANAGEMENT AND TRADE UNIONS

According to the provisions of the Law on Wholly Foreign-owned Enterprises, a wholly foreign-owned enterprise can decide the work environment and the staffing quotas on its own according to its production and operational needs, and submit the personnel plan to the relevant department. The enterprise may also recruit and engage staff with the assistance of the local department of personnel. If the need for engineering, technical and managerial personnel cannot be met in the locality, the enterprise may recruit from other parts of the country through consultation with the departments of personnel in different regions. The enterprise may dismiss staff who prove to be unsatisfactory after probation and training, or who are made redundant by changes in production and technical conditions. It may also take action against staff who break the rules and regulations of the enterprise. Depending on the seriousness of the offence, the staff members may be dismissed.

Staff have the right to set up a trade union to uphold their legitimate rights, and the enterprise must provide the conditions necessary for the trade union to carry out its activities. The trade union can sign the labour contract with the enterprise, on behalf of staff members, and supervise the execution of the contract. Conditions of employment, such as rewards and penalties, the salary system, welfare and benefits, labour protection and insurance, are the concern of the union. Representatives of the union have the right to attend discussions on the conditions of employment to convey the opinions of the staff members; they do not have voting rights. If the trade union considers that the decisions of the enterprise violate the law and the labour contract, the dispute can be handled through conciliation, arbitration or judicial procedures.

DURATION OF THE ENTERPRISE

The Law on Wholly Foreign-owned Enterprises stipulates that the term of operation of such an enterprise must be proposed by the foreign investor in the written application to establish the enterprise in the light of the specific conditions that apply to different enterprises and trades. Approval by the examination and approval body is required. The term of operation can be extended by filing an application for an extension with the approving body 180 days before expiry. The approval body must, within 30 days of receiving the application, determine whether or not to approve the extension.

A wholly foreign-owned enterprise subject to any of the following circumstances must terminate its business operations and make a timely public announcement. Termination must occur if:

- the term of operation expires;
- business cannot be carried on because of *force majeure*;
- bankruptcy proceedings are initiated; or
- the foreign investor decides to dissolve the business because of poor operation and management resulting in serious losses. The enterprise must, within 15 days of the date of the public announcement, submit the procedures and principles of liquidation, and the names of candidates for appointment to the liquidation committee to the examination and approval body for verification and approval.

The liquidation committee consists of the legal representatives of the wholly foreign-owned enterprise, representatives of the creditors, representatives from the original approval authorities, and Chinese registered accountants and lawyers. Prior to the conclusion of the liquidation proceedings, the foreign investor cannot remit or transfer the enterprise's funds out of the territory of China, nor dispose of the enterprise's property privately.

Upon the conclusion of the liquidation, the wholly foreign-owned enterprise must cancel its registration with the State Administration for Industry and Commerce, and hand in the business licence for cancellation.

CONCLUSION

Wholly foreign-owned investment enterprises have many advantages in the sense that they are entirely controlled by the foreign partners and there is no need for interference from a local Chinese partner in respect of management issues. Nevertheless, many foreign investors prefer to have a local partner to help them understand the market situation and deal with problems which the Chinese partner is much better equipped to handle. The trade union can play an important role in organising and allocating tasks, and in coordinating the relationship between labour and capital. Chapter 10, Labour Management, gives further details on labour relations.

The liberalisation of investments involving wholly foreign-owned enterprises continues, with permission granted to establish consulting companies in Shanghai and wholly foreign-owned trading companies in the Wai Gao Qiao Special Bonded Zone Area of Pudong Shanghai. Such permissions, while now being granted on an experimental basis, could be the beginning of a much more liberal system for foreign investment generally in China.

CHAPTER 7
HOLDING COMPANIES

In recent times, some multinational corporations have been given approval by China's Ministry of Foreign Trade and Economic Cooperation (MOFTEC) to establish foreign-invested holding companies (also called umbrella companies), within the territory of the People's Republic of China. These holding companies are analogous to those common in Western countries, with some differences. After setting up some form of foreign-owned enterprise—an equity joint venture or a cooperative enterprise—multinational corporations often wish to establish holding companies. This is done to increase investment or to reinvest in China, as well as to coordinate and manage their investment companies already established in China.

To meet the needs of foreign investors and due to practical demands, China's foreign trade authorities have permitted some multinational corporations with considerable investment in China to establish holding companies. Also, the authorities have formulated Provisional Regulations on the Establishment of Investment Companies by Foreign Investors (the Provisional Regulations). In accordance with Article 1 of the Provisional Regulations, the holding company takes the form of a limited liability company. It can be in the form of a wholly foreign-owned enterprise or a Chinese–foreign joint venture.

CONDITIONS FOR ESTABLISHMENT

To establish a holding company, the following conditions must be met.

(1) The foreign investors must have a sound reputation. Their total assets during the year preceding the application cannot be less than US$400 million.

(2) The amount of the foreign investor's paid-up capital contribution must exceed US$10 million. Furthermore, approval must have been obtained for at least three project proposals of the investor's intended investment projects. Alternatively, the foreign investor must already have established more than 10 foreign-invested

enterprises in the People's Republic of China: these must be engaged in production or infrastructure construction and the total amount of the paid-up capital contribution of the registered capital must exceed US$30 million.

(3) The registered capital of the holding company cannot be less than US$30 million.

APPROVAL PROCEDURES

To apply for the establishment of a holding company, the investor must submit the following documents to MOFTEC for examination and approval. The investor must already have the consent of the relevant foreign trade and economic cooperation authorities.

(1) If the holding company is to be in the form of an equity joint venture, the investor submits the project proposal and the feasibility study, contract and articles of association signed by the parties to the holding company.

(2) If the holding company is to be established in the form of a wholly foreign-owned enterprise, the investor submits the project proposal, the wholly foreign-owned enterprise application form, feasibility study and the articles of association signed by the foreign investor.

(3) The certificate (in duplicate) establishing the credit rating of each investing party, the registration certificate, and duplicate copies of the legal representative certificate (a legal document confirming that the person signing documents on behalf of the company has the legal right to do so, conferred, for example, by a resolution of the board).

(4) The approval certificate(s) (duplicate) for the enterprise(s) already invested in by the foreign investor, the business licence (duplicate) and the capital verification report (duplicate) issued by certified public accountants registered in China.

(5) The balance sheet of each investing party for the previous three years.

(6) Other documents as required by the approval authorities.

All of the above-mentioned documents must be the original copies except those specified as duplicate.

TERMS OF OPERATION

The terms of operation of a holding company are examined and approved in accordance with the relevant State regulations. Upon approval by the People's Bank of China, the company may provide financial support for the enterprises in which it has investments.

The establishment of an enterprise in which the holding company invests must be approved in accordance with the limited authorisation and approval procedures for foreign-invested enterprises. The company and its enterprises are legal entities independent of each other. Their business transactions shall be dealt with as normal business transactions between independent enterprises.

BUSINESS SCOPE

A holding company may invest in fields such as industry, agriculture, infrastructure, energy, etc., where foreign investment is encouraged or permitted by the State. With the written authorisation of the enterprises for which it is the umbrella company (and with the consensus of the board of directors), a holding company may provide the following services for such enterprises:

(1) to assist, or act as an agent, in purchasing machinery, equipment and office appliances for their own use, and to assist, or act as an agent, in purchasing raw materials, components and parts used by the enterprises for their own production for domestic or overseas markets, as well as to distribute the products in both the domestic and international markets, and to provide after-sales services;

(2) to balance foreign exchange revenue and expenditure among the enterprises with the consent and under the supervision of the foreign exchange administration authorities;

(3) to assist the enterprises in the recruitment and employment of personnel and to provide technical training, market promotion and consulting; and

(4) to assist the enterprises in seeking loans and to provide guarantees.

A holding company may provide consulting services for its investors.

INVESTMENT ENTERPRISES OF THE HOLDING COMPANY

A holding company may invest in the fields outlined above. The investment enterprises through which it operates include:

- enterprises in which the holding company invests directly or jointly with other foreign investors and/or Chinese investors, and the capital contribution of the holding company together with other foreign investors accounts for more than 25% of the registered capital of such enterprises already established; and

- enterprises already established within the territory of China in which the capital contribution of the holding company and the other foreign investors accounts for more than 25% of the registered capital as a result of taking over part or all of the share from its investors, or its affiliated companies or other foreign investors.

According to Article 5 of the Provisional Regulations, a holding company enjoys the preferential treatment of a foreign-invested enterprise, and is issued a foreign-invested enterprise approval certificate and a foreign-invested enterprise business licence.

CONCLUSION

It is important to note that while the holding company vehicle has provided many multinationals with a structure in China through which to operate nationally, the actual functions of a holding company are rather limited.

According to MOFTEC provisions, a holding company may act mainly as a vehicle for investing in subsidiaries which must each be dealt with as a separate legal entity. Therefore, a holding company is not permitted to provide foreign exchange balancing especially where State administration of exchange controls are required. In addition, inter-company financing can only be provided if the holding company is approved as a finance company. To date, such approvals have been very limited.

Nevertheless, for many companies, particularly multinationals positioning for the long term in the China market, the holding company enables the establishment of a national presence and the advantage of centralised management teams.

PART 3
OPERATIONAL ISSUES

CHAPTER 8

MANAGEMENT OF JOINT VENTURES

The management of a joint venture is often a very difficult task because you are dealing with parties from not only two different legal entities, but two different cultures which may have a different perception altogether on how the joint venture should be managed. Generally, Chinese State-owned enterprises have a completely different management style from that of Western enterprises; in the past this style was more political than commercial. At the same time, foreign investors are coming into China with very commercial ideas and with certain parameters and time-frames in which to develop their investment.

This chapter sets forth the basic structure and operational parameters within which the management of a joint venture should conduct its operations.

BOARD OF DIRECTORS

The highest authority of a joint venture is its board of directors, which decides all major issues. The number of directors from each party and the composition of the board are stipulated in the contract and articles of association after consultation among the parties to the venture.

In order to comply with the requirements of the Joint Venture Law, the board of directors cannot have less than three members. The allocation of directors is determined after consultation among the parties to the venture in accordance with the proportion of investment subscribed by each party.

Directors are appointed by the parties to the joint venture. The chairman of the board is appointed after consultation and may come from either side. The term of office for directors is four years; their term of office may be extended.

Meetings of the Board of Directors

The board of directors must convene at least once every year. The meeting is called and presided over by the chairman of the board. Should the chairman be unable to call the meeting, he should authorise the vice-chairman or a director to call and preside over the meeting.

The chairman may convene an interim meeting at the suggestion of more than one-third of the directors. A board meeting requires a quorum of two-thirds or more of the directors. Should a director be unable to attend, he may appoint a proxy to represent him and vote in his stead. A board meeting is usually held at the joint venture's legal address.

The chairman of the board is the legal representative of the joint venture. Should the chairman be unable to perform his duties, he should authorise the vice-chairman of the board or a director to represent the joint venture.

Procedures for Meetings

The rules of procedure are formulated in accordance with the relevant law, such as the Joint Venture Law and the Law on Cooperative Joint Ventures, and their respective implementing regulations, and the articles of association of the joint venture, and must fully reflect the opinions and requirements of the parties. Decisions on the following matters can be made only after having been unanimously agreed upon by the directors present at a board meeting:

- amendment to the articles of association of the joint venture;
- suspension or dissolution of the joint venture;
- increase in or assignment of the registered capital of the joint venture; and
- merger of the joint venture with other economic organisations.

Decisions on other matters may be made according to the rules of procedure stipulated in the articles of association. These may say that decisions can be made after having been agreed upon by all the directors, two-thirds of the directors, or simply more than half the directors.

MANAGEMENT STRUCTURE

A joint venture should establish a management office responsible for day-to-day management and operations: it should have a general manager and several deputy general managers who assist the general manager in his work.

General Manager

The general manager carries out the decisions of the board and organises and conducts the day-to-day management and operations of the joint venture. Within the scope of authorisation by the board, the general manager represents the joint venture; internally, he has the right to appoint and dismiss his subordinates and exercise other powers authorised by the board. The specific extent of his authority is stipulated in the contract and articles of association of the joint venture.

Deputy General Managers

In handling major issues, the general manager consults with the deputy general managers. Depending on the particular circumstances, the contract and articles of association should specify which matters the general manager can decide on and which he can decide on after consulting with the relevant deputy general manager or managers.

The general manager and deputy general managers are recommended by the parties to the joint venture and engaged by the board of directors. These positions may be held either by Chinese or foreign citizens.

If the board of directors so determines, the chairman, vice-chairman or other directors of the board may concurrently be the general manager, deputy general managers or other high-ranking managerial personnel of the joint venture.

CONFLICTS OF INTEREST AND COMPLIANCE WITH THE LAW

The general manager or deputy general managers cannot hold posts concurrently as general manager or deputy general managers of other enterprises. They should not get involved in other economic organisations' commercial competition against their own joint venture. The general manager, deputy general managers and other high-ranking managerial personnel should strictly comply with Chinese law. Graft or serious dereliction of duty on the part of the general manager, deputy general managers or other high-ranking managerial personnel may lead to their dismissal at any time by a decision of the board of directors.

CONCLUSION

Particular attention should be paid to management issues when setting up a joint venture in China. When joint ventures run into management problems, it is usually as a result of factors discussed above. It is important also that one party has clear management control or that management of various aspects of the joint venture are clearly defined in the contract and articles of association. In this way, disputes and clashes between the parties can be avoided or minimised.

CHAPTER 9
CUSTOMS DUTIES

All goods imported into or exported out of the People's Republic of China are subject to customs duties, including goods originally produced or manufactured in China but purchased outside of China and imported. The key legislation governing the levy of customs is the Customs Law and the Regulations on Import and Export Tariff of the People's Republic of China (the Customs Import and Export Tariff). The regulations were promulgated by the State Council on 7 March 1985; they were amended and promulgated on 12 September 1987, then amended and promulgated a second time on 18 March 1992.

TARIFF COMMISSION

The Tariff Commission was established by the State Council and charged with the responsibility to:

* formulate guidelines, policies and principles;
* draw up and/or amend the Regulations on the Customs Import and Export Tariff;
* examine the draft of amendments to tariff rates;
* set temporary tariff rates; and
* examine and approve the partial adjustment to the tariff rates.

The composition of the Tariff Commission is prescribed by the State Council. Regulations on the levy of import duties on an incoming passenger's luggage and articles, and on personal postal matters, are formulated by the Tariff Commission. The agent entrusted to go through the related customs procedures shall abide by all provisions of the present regulations that apply to his client. Both the consignee of imports and the consignor of exports are obliged to pay customs duties.

TARIFF RATES

Tariff rates on imports are based on either general rates or preferential rates. General rates, for the purpose of taxation, apply to goods imported from, and produced or manufactured in, countries or regions with which China has no agreement for reciprocal tariff preference. Preferential rates apply to goods imported from, and produced or manufactured in, countries or regions with which China has concluded such agreements.

Subject to special approval by the Tariff Commission, preferential rates may be applied to imported goods to which general rates would otherwise apply. A special duty may be imposed on goods imported from any country or region which imposes a discriminating duty or effects other forms of discriminating treatment in respect of imported goods originating in China. The goods subject to the imposition of the special duty, its rates, and the dates of its introduction and discontinuation are determined by the Tariff Commission and promulgated for enforcement.

Imported and exported goods are classified under an appropriate heading or subheading according to interpretation rules set out in the Customs Import and Export Tariff. Tariff rates are applied accordingly.

Customs duties are levied on imports or exports at the tariff rates in effect on the date of declaration by the consignee or consignor or his agent. Imports which may be declared prior to their entry are subject to import duties at the rates in effect on the date of entry. The rates in effect on the date when the imports or exports are first declared for importation or exportation apply in the recovery or refund of duties. Specific provisions in this respect are formulated by Customs General Administration.

Assessment of Duty Payable

The amount of duty payable on goods to be imported is assessed according to the CIF price based on the transaction value verified by Customs. The CIF price covers the cost of the goods, packing charges, freight, insurance premiums and other service charges incurred prior to the unloading of the goods in China. If the CIF price cannot be ascertained after examination by Customs, duty is assessed by Customs on the basis of the following prices in order of precedence:

- the transaction value of the identical or similar goods imported from the same country or area;

- the transaction value of the identical or similar goods on the international market;

- the wholesale price of the identical or similar goods on the domestic market, less the import duties levied and other taxes collected in the process of importation, the charges on transportation and storage after importation, the business expenses and the profits; or

- the value assessed by Customs by means of other reasonable methods.

(1) The duty-paying value of mechanical appliances, vehicles or any other goods which must be shipped out of China for the purpose of repairs with the declaration for exports made in advance and shipped back into China within the time limit set by Customs will be identical with the charges on the repairs and the cost of materials and spare parts used for the repairs. Both will be subject to examination and approval by Customs.

(2) The duty-paying value of goods shipped out of China for processing overseas with the declaration for exports made to Customs in advance and shipped back into China within the time limit set by Customs will be identical with the difference between the CIF price of the processed goods at the time of entry and the CIF price of the original goods shipped out of China or of identical or similar goods at the time of entry. The description of the goods to which this applies and the specific measures for their regulation are provided separately by the Customs General Administration.

(3) The duty-paying value of goods imported on lease (including for rent) is assessed according to the rental for the goods, and is subject to examination and approval by Customs.

(4) The duty-paying value of goods imported includes payments of charges and fees made to parties outside ˚China for patents, trademarks, copyrights, know-how, computer software and information for the purpose of their production, use, publication or circulation in China.

(5) The duty-paying value of goods exported for sale is identical with the FOB price of the goods with the export duties deducted. The above FOB price is subject to examination and approval by Customs; if the FOB price cannot be ascertained, the value will be assessed by Customs.

(6) The consignors or consignees of imported or exported goods or their agents are obliged to declare to Customs the true transaction

value of the goods. If the declared value is lower or higher than the transaction value of identical or similar goods, the duty-paying value will be determined by Customs in accordance with the relevant provisions of the current regulations.

(7) The consignee of imports or consignor of exports or his agent, will, at the time he submits the declaration for imports or exports, produce to Customs the invoices indicating the actual price, freight, insurance premiums and other expenses incurred by the goods (with manufacturers' invoices, if any), packing lists and other relevant papers for their examination and approval. All invoices and papers must be signed and stamped by the consignee or consignor or his agent to the effect that they are true and correct. If necessary, Customs may examine the relevant contracts, accounts, bills and other papers of both the buyers and the sellers or make any further investigation. Customs may also check the above documents and papers even after the levy of customs duties and the release of the goods.

(8) In case the CIF price of imports, the FOB price of exports, the rental for imported or exported goods, the charges on repairs or the cost of materials and spare parts are in foreign currencies, they will be converted into Renminbi at a price halfway between the buying and selling prices quoted by the State administrative body in charge of exchange control on the date of issue of the Notice of Duty. Customs may apply the exchange rate set by the administrative body.

Payment, Refund and Recovery of Customs Duties

The consignee or consignor or his agent must pay customs duties at the designated bank within seven days (excluding Sundays and national holidays) of Customs issuing the Notice of Duty. If any payments are in arrears, Customs may order the payment of the current duties plus 1% of the amount in arrears every day after the eighth day until the amount in arrears is paid in full.

Customs can choose to levy customs duties and charge fees for delayed payment in Renminbi. Customs can issue receipts for duties collected or late payment of fees: receipts follow the form prescribed by the Customs General Administration. In any of the following situations, the consignee or consignor or his agent may, within one year of the date of payment of customs duties, claim a refund by submitting to Customs a written application attaching the receipt. If:

- an excessive amount of customs duty has been paid as a result of wrong assessment by Customs;
- any goods on which duty has been paid and which were exempt from examination by Customs, and are subsequently discovered to be shortlanded (verification by Customs is required); or
- any goods for export on which duty has been paid and then are not shipped for some reason and are declared to Customs as shut-out cargo (verification by Customs is required).

Customs should reply in writing within 30 days of receiving the application for the refund notifying the applicant of its decision. If customs duties are short-levied or not levied, Customs can, within one year of the date of payment of customs duties or the date of release of the goods, recover the amount of duty outstanding. If any imports or exports are short-levied or not levied owing to a violation of Customs regulations by the consignee or consignor or his agent, Customs can recover the customs duties within three years.

Reductions or Exemptions

Customs duties will be reduced or exempted on goods and articles in accordance with the relevant provisions of the international treaties to which the People's Republic of China is a contracting or acceding party. Regulations on the levying or exemption of customs duties on free replacement goods are separately formulated by the Customs General Administration.

Exempted goods

Goods falling into any of the following categories may be exempted from the levy of Customs duties upon verification by Customs:

- a consignment of goods on which customs duties payable are estimated to be below RMB 10 yuan;
- advertising matter and samples which are of no commercial value;
- materials which are rendered gratis by international organisations or foreign governments; and
- fuels, stores, beverages and provisions for use *en route* loaded on any means of transport in transit across the frontier.

Reimportation and re-exportation of goods

If any goods exported should be shipped back into China for some reason, the original consignor or his agent should submit a declaration for entry with the original documents and papers attached and verified by Customs. Import duties may not be levied but export duties already paid will not be refunded.

If any goods imported should be shipped back out of China for some reason, the original consignee or his agent should submit a declaration for return with the original documents and papers attached and verified by Customs. Export duties may not be levied but import duties already collected will not be refunded.

Machinery for construction, engineering vehicles and vessels and the like that are temporarily admitted with a time-limit that is subsequently extended upon approval by Customs, are subject to the levy of import duties for the duration of the extension. Specific measures are separately prepared by the Customs General Administration.

Import duties on raw materials, subsidiary materials, spare parts, accessories, components and packing materials imported for processing or assembling, or for the manufacture of goods to be exported, may be exempted. Alternatively, import duties may be collected upon importation and then be refunded in accordance with the quantities of the finished products actually exported.

Damaged goods

Customs may, in consideration of the circumstances, grant a reduction or exemption of customs duties on any goods falling into any of the following categories:

- goods damaged, destroyed or lost *en route* to China or at the time of unloading;

- goods damaged, destroyed or lost by *force majeure* after unloading but prior to release; and

- goods discovered already leaky, damaged or rotten at the time of examination by Customs, provided that the cause proves to be other than improper storage.

Temporary exemptions

The levy of customs duties may be exempted temporarily on samples, exhibits, engineering equipment and vehicles for construction, instruments and tools for installation, cinematographic and television apparatus, containers of goods, and theatrical costumes and paraphernalia, provided that a deposit of an amount to that of the customs duties or a guarantee bond is submitted to Customs by the consignee or consignor.

The time-limit for such temporary shipping into or out of China is six months, but may be extended at the discretion of Customs.

Designated areas

Customs duties are reduced or exempted on goods receiving preferential treatment and on goods imported into or exported out of the designated areas, such as:

- Special Economic Zones; and
- designated enterprises (such as Chinese–foreign equity joint ventures, Chinese–foreign cooperative joint ventures and wholly foreign-owned enterprises).

Applications for Reductions or Exemptions

If the consignee or consignor or his agent applies for *ad hoc* reduction or exemption of customs duties on imports or exports, a written application giving valid reasons and accompanied by the necessary documentary evidence should be submitted to Customs for examination prior to the importation or exportation of the goods.

Customs will transmit the verified application to Customs General Administration, which may, in accordance with the relevant regulations formulated by the State Council, examine and approve it with or without consulting the Ministry of Finance.

Imported goods that are given tariff preference for reduction or exemption of duties should, in case of their being sold, transferred, or devoted to other use upon approval by Customs within the period of its supervision, be subject to recovery of duties based on their value taking into account depreciation. The period of supervision should be separately stipulated by the Customs General Administration.

PROCEDURES FOR APPEAL

Those who disagree with the decision taken by Customs on the collection, reduction, recovery or refund of duties must first pay the duties and then, within 30 days of the issue of the Notice of Duty, submit a written application to Customs for a reconsideration of the case. Late applications will not be considered. Customs should make its decision on the appeal within 15 days of receipt of the application.

Should the person obliged to pay customs duties refuse to accept the decision, he may appeal to the Customs General Administration for reassessment within 15 days of receiving the note on the decision.

The Customs General Administration should make its decision on the appeal within 30 days.

Should the person obliged to pay customs duties find the decision made by the Customs General Administration unacceptable, he may bring the case to the People's Court within 15 days of receiving the note of decision.

PENALTIES

Any act in violation of the present regulations which constitutes the crime of smuggling, or of the regulations on Customs supervision and control, will be dealt with in accordance with *The Customs Law of the People's Republic of China*, Implementing Regulations on Imposing Administrative Penalties under *The Customs Law of the People's Republic of China* and other relevant laws and regulations.

Customs, in accordance with the relevant regulations, rewards anyone who provides information or assistance leading to the uncovering of any evasion of customs duties in violation of the rules. All information is kept confidential.

CONCLUSION

It is critical that both investors and traders develop good relations with the customs authorities in China as these authorities can be both a help and a hindrance.

All products exported from China and all raw materials imported for production must go through Customs. The customs authorities take a very strict view on smuggling activities, and investors should be aware that smuggling carries with it severe fines and penalties. It is therefore important to understand current duties and rates: long-term successful investment and trading activities in China can be enjoyed by investors who work within the parameters of the customs system.

CHAPTER 10
LABOUR MANAGEMENT

Because of China's historical socialist background and the importance which such a philosophy places upon labour rights, China has, in the course of its economic growth, developed a detailed series of laws and regulations addressing labour concerns.

While one of the most attractive incentives for foreign investors to invest in China is the availability of cost-effective labour sources, one must be aware that the government strictly regulates the use of labour to avoid exploitation of Chinese people by foreign entities or governments. After all, such exploitation was one of the key reasons for China's wars of resistance against both the colonial powers and the Japanese, culminating in the liberation of China by the Communist Party in 1949.

The existing legislation governing labour matters is extensive. *The Labour Law of the People's Republic of China* adopted by the People's National Congress in 1949 serves as the basis of all principles governing labour protection. A distinctive aspect of the Labour Law is the creation of employment, which is important in a socialist country with such a vast population. There are strict regulations on working hours, rest-days and holidays, protection of female workers and underaged workers (who were exploited before 1949), methods of dealing with labour disputes, and on supervision and inspection of labour.

The Labour Law applies broadly to all enterprises and individuals hiring staff or workers within China. This means that the law covers the representative offices of foreign investment enterprises as well as domestic entities.

One of the fundamental rights of workers in China is the right to join or organise trade unions and, according to the Labour Law, to 'participate in democratic management through workers congress, workers representative assembly or other forums, or consultation on the basis of equality of his/her employer unit concerning the protection of his/her legal rights and interest'. This clause causes some concern for foreign investors, particularly those coming from countries where strikes often cripple business. Nevertheless, the Chinese authorities view it prudent to include such clauses in the legislation to avoid exploitation and to protect workers.

An enterprise is required to provide support to workers to organise trade unions and to provide conditions for the launching of trade union activities in accordance with *The Trade Union Law of the People's Republic of China*. A trade union has the right to represent workers in the presentation of demands for increased wages and salaries, and improved living and welfare treatment and labour conditions.

A trade union may also monitor an enterprise's compliance with labour laws and regulations. Where it is found to have violated the law, immediate sanctions may be imposed and the enterprise investigated. Where no action has been taken, a report may be made to the Labour Administration Office and other relevant bodies while corrective measures are undertaken.

The following laws and regulations govern labour matters, particularly in relation to foreign investment enterprises:

- *The Labour Law of the People's Republic of China*;
- *The Trade Union Law of the People's Republic of China*;
- Notice of the Ministry of Labour, the Ministry of Public Security and the All-China Federation of Trade Unions concerning strengthening Labour Management in Foreign Investment Enterprises and Private Enterprises and the Effective Safeguarding of the Legal Rights and Interests of Employees;
- Regulations on the Right of Autonomy of Foreign Investment Enterprises in the Hiring of Personnel and on Employees' Wages, Insurance and Welfare Expenses;
- Implementation of the Right of Autonomy of Foreign Investment Enterprises in their Use of Personnel; and
- Regulations concerning the Labour Protection of Female Staff and Workers.

ENGAGEMENT AND DISMISSAL OF STAFF

On 10 November 1986, the Ministry of Labour and Personnel issued the Regulations on the Right of Autonomy of Foreign Investment Enterprises in the Hiring of Personnel and on Employees' Wages, Insurance and Welfare Expenses.

These regulations were formulated to implement the State Council Regulations concerning Encouragement of Foreign Investment, to guarantee the right of autonomy of foreign investment enterprises in the hiring of personnel, and to appropriately determine the wages, insurance and welfare expenses of Chinese employees.

A foreign investment enterprise may, in accordance with its production and operational requirements, determine its own organisational structure and personnel system. With the assistance of the local department of labour, it may recruit staff based on an examination of the best candidates.

Should engineering and technical personnel or operations and management personnel required by a foreign investment enterprise be unavailable locally, they may be recruited from other districts subject to the approval of the departments of labour and personnel of those districts.

If a foreign investment enterprise decides to engage currently employed engineering and technical personnel, or operations and management personnel, their original work units must support and permit the transfer. In the event of a dispute, the local department of labour and personnel will adjudicate.

Senior management personnel appointed by the Chinese party to positions in a foreign investment enterprise should be qualified, familiar with technology and have management capability, and should also be able to cooperate and work with foreigners. Their departments should support them in their work and not transfer them to another post during their term of office. If a transfer is necessary, the approval of the board of directors will need to be obtained.

Personnel may be dismissed who are found to be substandard following a probationary or training period, or who are made redundant as a result of changes in an enterprise's production technology. Employees who violate the rules and regulations of an enterprise may, depending on the seriousness of the circumstances, be penalised or even dismissed.

LABOUR PROTECTION

An enterprise is required to recruit workers in accordance with State labour laws and policy regulations. It cannot recruit peasant labour without authorisation, or recruit female labour for certain posts: it is also forbidden to recruit child labour.

An enterprise may not take money or goods as a 'factory entry pledge' and will not take custody of or keep as a pledge any residency permit, short-term residency permit or other document verifying personal status. Where documents such as residency permits have been held in custody or taken as pledges without authorisation, or money (goods) have been received as pledges, the Public Security Office and the Labour Supervisory Office can order their immediate return.

The State has special labour protection measures for female workers and underage workers. Underage workers are those workers who are over 16 years and under 18 years of age. Female workers cannot work in mines, engage in extremely strenuous physical labour, or do any kind of work female workers should avoid. During their menstrual periods, female workers must not work at high altitudes, in low temperatures or do work which involves contact with cold water.

Pregnant workers must not engage in strenuous physical labour, or do any kind of work that should be avoided during pregnancy. No extra hours or night shifts can be worked by female workers at or past the seventh month of pregnancy. Maternity leave for female workers must be at least 90 days. During the infant-feeding period allowed to female workers with a baby under one year of age, no work can be allocated to the mothers; no extra hours or night shifts are allowed either.

Underage workers are not allowed to work in mines, work with poisonous or harmful substances, undertake intense physical labour, or do any other kind of work such workers should avoid. An employer should arrange regular health checks for underage workers

WAGES, INSURANCE AND WELFARE BENEFITS

The wage levels of employees of foreign investment enterprises are determined by the board of directors. The general principle is that the wages of workers in a foreign investment enterprise should not be less than 120% of the average wage of employees of local State-run enterprises engaged in a similar industry.

Such wages will also need to be adjusted progressively in accordance with the economic performance of the enterprise and with the State consumer price index. If the economic performance is good, wage levels may be increased significantly. However, if the economic performance is poor, they may be slightly raised or even not increased at all.

Wages and Salaries

Wages must be paid in accordance with the principle of 'to each according to his work' and based on equal pay for equal work. The State exercises macro-control over the national payroll. An enterprise may, in accordance with the circumstances of its production and business operations and its results, independently determine its own wage distribution system and wage levels.

The State implements a minimum wage protection system. Specific standards for minimum wages are determined by the provincial, autonomous regional and directly administered municipal people's governments. When determining and adjusting wage levels, the following factors should be taken into consideration:

- the minimum living expenses of workers and the average minimum living expenses of their dependants;
- the average wage for the region and for the particular industry;
- labour productivity;
- employment situation; and
- differences in the levels of economic development between different regions.

Wages must be paid to workers in cash on a monthly basis. Deductions or delays in payment without proper reason are not permitted. An enterprise must pay its workers' wages in full, on time and in a monetary form, and may not embezzle wages or pay them in arrears. Where an enterprise worker's wage is lower than the lowest wage regulated by State and local governments or a worker's salary is embezzled, the Labour Supervisory Office may order the enterprise to make up the amount and may also impose a fine in accordance with the law.

Insurance and Welfare Benefits

A foreign investment enterprise must pay old-age pension funds and unemployment insurance funds for Chinese employees in accordance with the provisions of the local people's government. Insurance and welfare benefits for employees during their term of employment for medical treatment, industrial accident and maternity leave, should be paid according to the relevant provisions of the Chinese Government for State-run enterprises. Expenses incurred must be paid from the enterprise's funds strictly in accordance with the needs of the situation.

A foreign investment enterprise will also be required to disburse a housing subsidy fund in accordance with the provisions of the local people's government, to be used by the Chinese party to the enterprise to subsidise the construction and purchase of housing for employees.

WORK HOURS

An enterprise must strictly implement the State-regulated system of work hours and leave. The State provides that each worker can work no more than eight hours a day, with average weekly working hours not exceeding 44 hours. An employer must ensure that every worker has at least two rest-days each week. For production line workers working on a piece-work basis, the employer, bearing in mind the maximum number of hours that by law an employee is obliged to work, may determine work quotas and adopt piece-work rates for the workers. An employer must arrange for workers to have statutory holidays on the following festivals:

- New Year's Day;
- Traditional Spring Festival;
- International Labour Day;
- National Day; and
- other festivals which are holidays as stipulated by laws and regulations of the State.

An employer must pay its workers wages that are higher than the normal wage rates for normal working hours:

- when arranging overtime, not less than 150% of the normal wage must be paid;
- when arranging work during rest-days and where such rest-days cannot be postponed and taken at another time, not less than 200% of the normal wage must be paid; and
- when arranging work during an official public holiday, not less than 300% of the normal wage must be paid.

An enterprise may extend work hours due to production and business requirements following union agreement and consultation with workers. However, such extension must not exceed three hours per day, and not exceed 44 hours per month. An enterprise must remunerate workers for overtime worked in accordance with State regulations. Where an enterprise forces workers to work extra shifts and extra hours in violation of State regulations, a worker may refuse to do so. The enterprise may not reduce that worker's wages and, further, not use this as a reason for dismissing him.

LABOUR CONTRACTS

A labour contract is defined in the Labour Law as 'an agreement made between a worker and an employer unit to establish a work-based relationship and to define the rights and obligations of both parties' and is necessary in any situation involving employment of labour. Without a labour contract there can be no employer–employee relationship. Conclusion of and amendment to a labour contract must be on the basis of equality, voluntary participation and mutual consent, and must not be in violation of the principles of law or statutory regulations.

Following the signing of a labour contract, certification by the local Labour Administration Office will be undertaken. Where State regulations have not been complied with, the Labour Supervisory Office may order revocation of the recruitment of employees and impose fines for corruption.

A labour contract, once signed, immediately becomes legally binding on the parties. There is no separate approval requirement for such contracts.

Invalid Labour Contracts

The following are not recognised under law:

- a labour contract which is in violation of the provisions of laws and statutory regulations; and
- a labour contract concluded through means of deception, threat or other unlawful means.

An invalid labour contract has no legal binding force. Where part of a labour contract is invalid, it does not affect other parts of the contract, which remain valid. Either the labour disputes arbitration committee or the People's Court have the power to review and determine under law the validity or otherwise of a labour contract.

Contract Terms

A labour contract must be concluded in writing; oral contracts are not binding. In order to be binding, a labour contract must specify the:

- duration of the contract;
- work tasks;
- labour protection measures and labour conditions;
- labour remuneration;
- labour discipline;
- conditions for termination of contract; and
- responsibility for breach of contract.

These are the minimum requirements in a labour contract; other items may be added after negotiation. The duration may be flexible, have a fixed time-limit, or depend on a certain amount of work to be fulfilled.

Most labour contracts stipulate a probationary period; the maximum probationary period is six months. It is recommended that a long probationary period be adopted so that foreign employers can get to see the real work attributes of their staff before confirmation. The parties to a labour contract may include terms concerning the keeping of commercial secrets: this is particularly important to companies engaged in technology transfer work.

Terminating a Contract

The parties to a labour contract may terminate it subject to agreement. An employer has the right to terminate it in any of the following circumstances:

- where it is proved, on the expiry of the probationary period, that a worker has failed to meet employment requirements;
- where a worker has seriously violated labour discipline or the rules and regulations of the employer unit;
- where a worker has committed serious dereliction of his duties or has practised favouritism or other irregularities resulting in serious losses being incurred by the employer unit; or
- where a worker has been accused of criminal liability under the law.

In any of the following circumstances, an employer may rescind a labour contract. However, written notice must be provided to a worker, in person, 30 days in advance:

- where, after undergoing a period of medical treatment, a worker with an illness or non-work-related injury is unable to perform his original work duties and is also unable to perform another job arranged by the employer unit;
- where a worker is not competent to perform the job and remains unqualified even after training or being moved to another post; or
- where a labour contract can no longer be implemented due to major changes in the conditions that were relied on as the basis for concluding the contract and where an agreement to amend the labour contract cannot be reached by either party.

An employer may not terminate a labour contract in any of the following circumstances:

- where a worker suffers from an occupational disease or a work-related injury and has been confirmed as being totally or partially unable to work;

- where a worker suffers from an illness or injury for which medical treatment within a stipulated period is allowed;

- where a female worker is pregnant, on maternity leave or within the stipulated period for nursing; or

- in other circumstances as stipulated in laws and statutory regulations.

A worker may rescind a labour contract after informing the employer in writing 30 days in advance. A worker may, at any time, request the employer to terminate a contract in any of the following circumstances:

- during the probationary period;

- where an employer forces the worker to work through means of force, threat or illegal restriction of personal freedom; or

- where an employer fails to pay the remuneration or to provide the work conditions stipulated in the contract.

CONCLUSION

While one of the main advantages of, and incentives for, investing in China is the pool of low-cost labour, one should be aware that exploitation of labour is viewed very seriously by the authorities. The principles of a socialist economy specifically aim to protect labour rights. Therefore, it is advisable for foreign investors to pay careful attention to the regulations and enter into individual labour contracts wherever possible.

While the above chapter sets out the legal parameters within which to handle labour issues, one should be sensitive to the personality and cultural factors which are important in managing labour in China.

CHAPTER 11

TRADE

China has made great achievements in reviving its economy. The most progressive changes began 15 years ago when China opened to the outside world. Upon the founding of the People's Republic of China, foreign trade was chiefly regulated by direct administrative measures. Such methods were necessary in the early days of the new China and in the planned economy period, and were effective, as China's foreign trade was then limited in scale.

In the past, foreign trade in China was monopolised by a dozen or so State trading corporations. The monopoly has been gradually broken down since the inception of the open-door policy. The number of trading enterprises increased year by year and, as of 1996, has reached over 7000. The 15 years of reforms and open-door policy witnessed a great growth in foreign trade. China's imports and exports totalled US$195.72 billion in 1993, 575 times the 1949 figures of US$340 million, 172 times the 1950 sum of US$1,135 billion and 9.5 times the 1978 amount of US$20,638 billion. Today, China keeps trade ties with over 180 countries and regions in the world, and there are 180,000 Chinese enterprises across the country directly engaged in import and export operations.

Clearly, it is increasingly hard for administrative measures to effectively regulate such large-scale economic activities. China recognises that, to develop the national economy, it is necessary to bring the economy in line with international legal standards and practices. China has also repudiated the erstwhile diverse subsidy systems in foreign trade and clearly stipulated that foreign trade dealers have autonomy in management and must assume sole responsibility for profits and losses. The State policy for encouraging the development of foreign trade will be implemented by such incentives as setting up special monetary bodies to promote foreign trade, foreign trade development funds and risk funds, and export refunding.

As part of China's resolve to link its economy with that of the world, China now implements a unitary foreign trade system. The prohibition of or restrictions on imported and exported goods and technologies can only be made according to the Foreign Trade Law. These prohibitions and restrictions are entirely consistent with the General Agreement on Tariffs and Trade (GATT). Concerning the protection of domestic industries, China has repudiated import-substitution, administrative examination and approval and other systems, and adopted instead anti-dumping, countervailing and safeguarding measures that are internationally accepted.

As a result of opening to the outside world, the economy in China has boomed. Foreign trade made up merely 4.7% of GNP in 1978, only 10.8% in 1988, and is now as high as 38%. Most importantly, the economy in China will be managed according to GATT and a set of international trade rules. In 1986, China applied for the resumption of its contracting party status in GATT. As the basic GATT requirements embrace the unification and transparency of the trade system, a foreign trade law is vital.

FOREIGN TRADE LAW

It is expected that the Ministry of Foreign Trade and Economic Cooperation (MOFTEC) will spare no efforts to draft a series of administrative decrees and regulations. Already, in 1996, legislation has been enacted to regulate this area. There are regulations on the licence systems for foreign trade enterprises, regulations on the trade agency system, anti-dumping regulations, countervailing regulations, safeguarding measures, import and export chambers of commerce regulations, and regulations on controlling border trade, etc.

The new *Foreign Trade Law of the People's Republic of China*, passed on 12 May 1993 at the Seventh meeting of the Standing Committee of the Eighth National People's Congress, mainly deals with the import and export of commodities, the import and export of technologies, and the international services trade.

The Foreign Trade Law aims to develop foreign trade, maintain order in foreign trade activities and promote a healthy development of the socialist market economy. The term 'foreign trade' used in the Law refers to the import and export of goods and technologies and the international services trade: MOFTEC takes charge of all foreign trade in China.

The import and export of commodities are the most vital part of China's trade, while the import and export of technologies are simply the transference of such technologies. Both issues are dealt with in great detail in the Foreign Trade Law. However, as the international services trade is still a brand-new undertaking for China, involving a great many areas including finance, insurance, transportation, tourism, telecommunications, consulting services and engineering projects under contract, the Foreign Trade Law can only lay down a number of broad principles that must be followed in internationalising the trade system.

Principles and Policies

The Foreign Trade Law, as the fundamental law in the area of foreign trade, embodies the principles and policies that China has always insisted on in her foreign trade practice: equality, mutual benefit, unitary system, fairness and free will. It prescribes that:

(1) a foreign trade enterprise must go through the procedures of examination and approval;

(2) while making it possible to freely import and export most goods and technologies, quotas and licences must be used to control some of the items that have to be prohibited or restricted in import and export; and

(3) open and fair competition must be applied in the allotment of quotas.

China will gradually open its market according to international treaties and agreements it has concluded or acceded to, and will accord other contracting parties or participants market access nationally, as well as most favoured nation status. China also has the right to adopt, in accordance with the actual circumstances, corresponding measures against any country or region to counter their discriminatory banning, restrictions or other acts prejudicing Chinese goods.

In respect to anti-dumping, countervailing and safeguarding measures, the Chinese government will give appropriate assistance to related industries that suffer from inequitable foreign trade acts, or are overburdened by the international obligations to which China has committed.

Other measures will be taken to promote foreign trade including establishment of the Import and Export Bank, the trade development fund and the risks funds, the refund of duties on exports, and promotion of the development of consulting services. The State encourages every effort in trade development, helps to bring the initiative of the localities into play, and safeguards the autonomy of trade operators.

Foreign Trade Operator

The term 'foreign trade operator' used in the Law refers to a legal entity or organisation engaging in foreign trade activities in compliance with its provisions. A foreign trade operator engaging in the import and export of goods or technologies is required to meet the following requirements and get the licence from the department in charge of foreign economic cooperation and trade under the State Council.

(1) It must have its own name and organisational set-up.

(2) It must have a clearly defined scope of foreign trade operations.

(3) It must have the site, funds and professional personnel necessary for carrying out foreign trade activities.

(4) The import and export operations handled by its agencies must have reached the required standard or else it must have the necessary sources of goods for import or export.

(5) It must have fulfilled other conditions as required by other laws or administrative decrees.

The start-up and business operations of enterprises engaging in the international services trade must obey this and other relevant laws and administrative decrees. Foreign trade operators operate independently according to law and are responsible for their own profits or losses. In carrying out foreign trade activities, they should abide by contracts, ensure the quality of commodities and improve after-sales services.

An organisation or an individual that does not acquire a licence for carrying out foreign trade activities may entrust a foreign trade operator as agent to handle the *ad hoc* trade operations within the *ad hoc* scope of business. Foreign-funded enterprises (FFEs) are exempted from licences when importing non-productive goods for their own use, or equipment, raw and other materials needed for their own production purposes and for exporting their products.

A foreign trade operator acting as an agent must provide appropriate information to the trustor, such as market prices and client information. The trustor and the trustee sign a contract which stipulates the rights and obligations on both sides. The operator must provide documents and materials related to its foreign trade activities to the departments concerned which should undertake to protect the operator's commercial secrets.

IMPORT AND EXPORT OF GOODS AND TECHNOLOGIES

The State generally allows the free import and export of goods and technologies, except as otherwise provided for by laws and administrative decrees. It may restrict the import or export of goods or technologies:

- that involve national security and the public interest;
- that are in short supply domestically or are in danger of being exhausted;
- that are under restriction of import by those countries or regions importing them due to a limited market;
- to protect the smooth or accelerated development of certain industries at home;
- involving agricultural, animal husbandry and fishery products in any form;
- to maintain its financial position in the world or to control its balance of international payments; and
- according to international treaties or agreements to which it is a signatory or has acceded.

The State may ban the import or export of goods or technologies that:

- jeopardise national security or the public interest;
- endanger the life or health of the people;
- endanger the ecological environment; and
- fall under the provisions of international treaties or agreements to which it is a signatory or has acceded.

MOFTEC, together with other relevant departments under the State Council, may draw up, revise and publish the catalogues of goods and technologies whose import or export are restricted or banned. It may also, independently or jointly, take prompt decisions to restrict or ban the import or export of special goods or technologies.

Goods whose import or export is restricted are subject to quota or licence management; technologies are subject to licence management. Goods and technologies subject to quota or licence management can be imported or exported only when approved by the department in charge of foreign trade and economic cooperation independently or jointly with other relevant departments. The same bodies allocate import and export quotas. Allocations are in line with the import and export performances and capabilities of applicants and are made on the basis of the principles of efficiency, fairness, openness and fair competition.

CHINA'S CONTRACT LAW

The Foreign Economic Contract Law (the Contract Law) applies to economic contracts between enterprises or other economic organisations of China on the one hand, and foreign enterprises, other foreign economic organisations or individuals on the other. The exception is international transport contracts. The Law is implemented to protect the lawful rights and interest of the parties concerned and to promote the development of China's foreign economic relations.

All contracts made under the Contract Law should be based on the principles of equality and mutual benefit. Contracts for Chinese–foreign equity joint ventures, Chinese–foreign cooperative enterprises and Chinese-foreign cooperative exploitation and development of natural resources are to be performed in China. When disputes arise, the parties have the right to choose the law to be applied to the settlement. International practice may apply if no relevant provision is found in the Contract Law. Contracts made under the relevant laws and regulations of China can only be enforced upon prior approval by the relevant authorities of the State. Furthermore, the appendices listed in a contract form an integral part of the contract. Contracts concluded by means of fraud or under duress are invalid, and the party responsible for the invalidity of the contract is liable to reimburse the other party for any consequent loss.

Drafting Contractual Terms

In principle, a contract must state the following:

- the details of the parties including names, nationalities, principal place of business or residential addresses;
- the date and place for the signing of the contract;
- the type, kind and scope of the contract;
- technical conditions, quality, standards and specifications as well as quantities of the contract;
- time-limit, place and method of performance;
- terms of price, amount and terms of payment, and various additional charges;
- whether the contract could be assigned/transferred, or conditions for assignment;

- liabilities of and compensation to the parties for breach of contract;
- resolution of disputes; and
- languages to be used in the wording of the contract and effectiveness of such languages.

The limitations of risks borne by each party must also be stipulated in the contract. In respect of a long-term contract, the terms and conditions for extension and termination of the contract must be specified clearly. In addition, a guarantee clause for undertaking respective responsibilities should be included in the contract.

According to the Contract Law, a duly approved contract is legally binding. Both parties should fulfil their obligations as specified in the contract. If a party does not perform his contractual responsibilities, then that is recognised as a breach of contract, and the other party is entitled to ask for compensation for loss and damage. The method of calculating damages must be stipulated in the contract.

Disputes, *Force Majeure*, Amendments and Assignments

According to the Contract Law, disputes arising from a contract ought to be settled by the parties, if possible, through friendly consultation. If no settlement can be reached by consultation, each party is entitled to submit the dispute or controversy for arbitration in accordance with the arbitration clause set out in the contract.

Under the Law, if a party cannot perform its obligations within a time-limit due to *force majeure*, it should be relieved of its liability for delayed performance while the effects continue and no party is entitled to claim for damages for losses caused by *force majeure*. An event of *force majeure* means an occurrence and consequences which cannot be avoided and overcome, and which the parties could not foresee at the time of concluding the contract. It is recommended that a more precise definition of *force majeure* be specified in the contract.

Should a party wish to assign all or part of its equity to a third party, prior approval must be obtained from the other party. Furthermore, the approval of the original examination and approval authority must also be obtained.

Amendments to the contract may be made, but only come into force after a written agreement has been duly signed by both parties, and approval obtained from the original examination and approval authority. All kinds of notices or agreements for modification or cancellation of the contract must be in written form.

Terminations

The Contract Law stipulates that a contract may be terminated early when one of the following events occurs:

- the contract has already been performed in accordance with the contractual terms;
- the arbitration body or court decides to terminate the contract; or
- the parties to the contract agree to terminate it.

EXPERIMENTS IN COMPREHENSIVE TRADING

As an experiment, the China National Chemicals Import and Export Corporation (SINOCHEM), the country's biggest import and export trader, has been directed by the State Council to engage in comprehensive trading. To support the experiment, the China Foreign Economic and Trade Credit and Trust Investment Co. (CFETCTIC), which used to operate under MOFTEC, is now part of SINOCHEM. The experiment is to be carried out in the field.

Since 28 March 1995, the handling of foreign government loans, formerly handled by CFETCTIC, have been transferred to the Import and Export Bank of China, along with the relevant assets, debt rights and debts. This involves a total of US$12.7 billion including loans by the governments of Japan, Germany, Finland, Australia, Denmark, Kuwait and the North Europe Investment Bank under agreements signed by MOFTEC, and loans by Norway and Holland under agreements signed by CFETCTIC under the authorisation of MOFTEC.

As the pioneer in this kind of experiment, SINOCHEM aims to develop itself into an international conglomerate, with trading as its main business. It will also venture into industrial and technological development, financing and information technology. It expects to complete the process in three stages, within 10 years. For the first phase (1995–1996), the task is one of building up a framework for a comprehensive trading company and, at the same time, striving to turn SINOCHEM into a shareholding company by taking advantage of CFETCTIC's capabilities of commercial financing. The second phase covers the 1997–2000 period, during which SINOCHEM will be transformed into a comprehensive trading company highly competitive on the world market with sound trade, financing and real estate business. The last phase, to begin in 2001 and end in 2005, envisages the establishment of a system that streamlines oilfield exploitation, oil refining, oil storage and transport and petrochemicals production, as well as domestic and international marketing of the products. A comprehensive trade system will combine transit trading, import and export and domestic trade, and have the capacity to perform all functions of financing, based on non-bank financial institutions.

The SINOCHEM trading company will be modelled after Dae Woo of the Republic of Korea, to eventually become a multinational group with enough power to compete with any of its counterparts in the world. In 1994, SINOCHEM registered a business volume of US$15 billion to rank itself among the 30 largest companies of its kind in the world.

CONCLUSION

Trading rights have always remained the privilege of the domestic trading corporations. But, in response to interest expressed by foreign investors and as part of China's bid to enter the World Trade Organisation (WTO), the State Council recently announced policy changes to loosen this restriction. In 1996, the establishment of Chinese–foreign joint ventures for trading purposes was permitted in Shanghai's Pudong Special Zone; similar trading privileges have since been extended to the other Special Economic Zones. It is envisioned that further liberalisation (eventually permitting a very open and flexible trading system) will occur in conjunction with China's moves to enter WTO.

CHAPTER 12
RETAIL INDUSTRY

Long considered an area forbidden to foreign investment, the richly profitable retail business in China is now gradually opening up to foreigners. Since 1992, six big cities, including Beijing and Shanghai, and five Special Economic Zones, including Shenzhen and Hainan, have each opened two large Chinese–foreign joint venture shopping centres. So far China has approved some ventures to sell daily consumer goods, such as, the Yaohan Department Store in Pudong, Shanghai; the Yansha Shopping Centre in Beijing, and a joint venture set up by the Hong Kong Sun Hung Kai Properties and Beijing Dongan Market; more such approvals are expected soon.

In Beijing's busy Wangfujing Street, there are already two Chinese–foreign joint equity retailing shops of fairly large size, one with investment from the Hong Kong Pacific Group and the other from Germany. A joint cooperative shopping centre in the consulate district was funded by a Hong Kong company and is managed by the Hong Kong Yaohan group.

The country's main policies on the creation of Chinese–foreign joint equity ventures in the retail industry are that:

- imports shall not account for more than 30% of the goods sold by the business;
- generally, exports must be greater than imports to balance forex; and
- foreign-funded retail businesses must pay 3% of business turnover in business tax and 33% in income tax apart from paying tax on imported commodities.

The Chinese government realises that retail business directly affects the daily lives of the people and that it lacks experience in this area. Time is needed to acquire enough experience to avoid a zig-zag progression resulting from a rushed start. In fact, overseas cooperation is much needed in the development of the retail industry in China. Some of the foreign business investors have taken the approach of first developing real estate in China to get a firm foothold there and then cooperating with Chinese partners in retailing. A case in point is the project by Hong Kong New World Development to rebuild the Beijing Wangfujing Department Store.

Hong Kong business people are always seeking ways to establish a foothold in China's retail market. For example, Gold Lion has opened over 300 specialised outlets in different places in China to sell its products. Overseas business investors also contract for the management of retail shops. There is also the practice of legal entities on the mainland getting the licence for the shop but with funds largely coming from Hong Kong. Apart from stretching its tentacles to Beijing, the Hong Kong Pacific Group is reportedly planning to buy real estate in eight cities—Shanghai, Beijing, Tianjin, Nanjing, Wuhan, Ningbo, Hangzhou and Chengdu—on which to build department stores.

In addition, the Hong Kong Wing On International Group, Chuang's Group, and another group have set up specialist or chainstores with local department stores in Wuhan, Jinan and Shanghai. The Hong Kong Trade Development Council has been acting as a go-between by opening a trade exhibition, 'Hong Kong Show-Case', in Shenyang, Harbin and Zhenzhou to promote Hong Kong products in China.

OPENING UP TO FOREIGN PARTICIPATION

At present, only joint equity ventures are allowed to engage in retail and wholesale operations; solely foreign-owned commercial retail and wholesale enterprises are still not permitted to be set up in China, according to a recent announcement by the Ministry of Domestic Trade.

A pilot trial for foreign-funded commercial enterprises was started in the second half of 1992. It was then decided to run, on an experimental basis, one or two joint equity or cooperative commercial retail ventures each in Beijing, Shanghai, Tianjin, Guangzhou, Dalian, Qinghai and five Special Economic Zones. Since then, 14 joint equity retail ventures have been approved in China including four in Shanghai, two each in Beijing, Tianjin, Guangzhou and Qingdao, and one each in Dalian and Shantou with a total registered foreign capital of RMB 2 billion (foreign currency converted into Renminbi). Yansha in Beijing and Dongfang in Shanghai have become nationally noted bazaars.

Opening commercial enterprises to the outside world can only be achieved gradually. The aim is to upgrade present commercial facilities by importing foreign funds, and advanced foreign managerial and marketing experience and techniques. These would speed up the improvement in the overall strength of State commercial retail enterprises, widen marketing channels and promote exports through the efforts of overseas partners.

Chinese experts predict that there is great potential in China for developing the retail industry. In 1994, retail sales totalled RMB 1600 billion, 3.14 times the amount five years earlier. Presently, 130 bazaars each have sales topping RMB 100 million annually; there were just 10 bazaars of the same size 10 years ago.

TRIALLING FOREIGN-FUNDED ENTERPRISES

China intends to extend the scope for trialling retail joint ventures. Partners mostly from south-east and east Asian regions will be joined by partners from Western developed countries, according to a recent announcement by the International Department of the Ministry of Domestic Trade. The trials will be based upon experience gained through the trials of retail joint ventures in major Special Economic Zones and Chinese cities as described on p. 96.

China will step up the opening of the distribution sector to the outside world. The introduction of modern means of distribution such as chainstores, the goods delivering system and the agency system are being considered for joint equity and cooperative ventures. Where conditions permit, joint equity and cooperative wholesale ventures will be run on a trial basis.

One or two joint equity commercial ventures may be trialled in each of five Special Economic Zones and six coastal cities including Shanghai and Tianjin. Joint equity department stores which have been approved are entitled to import commodities valued at 30% of their annual turnover and may also export the same amount of commodities. These joint ventures can enjoy preferential terms accorded to foreign-funded enterprises such as the exemption for two years and reduction for three years of income tax.

Twelve joint equity retail ventures are so far operating in the Special Economic Zones and cities on a trial basis. The 12 joint ventures include Yansha and New Dong'an in Beijing, Huaxin in Tianjin, the First Yaohan, Dongfang, Runhua and Jiashike in Shanghai, Hualian–Broadway in Guangdong, Dalian Bazaar and Dalian Trading Building in Dalian, Baisheng First Department Store in Qingdao and the Gold–Silver Island Co. in Shantou. Cooperation with the CVIK Shopping Centre in Beijing will end, so the centre is not included on the trial list.

The 12 ventures in the trial are mostly retail shops with retail space ranging from 20,000 sq.m. to 150,000 sq.m. So far, only

Dongfang and Yansha are operating. A long construction period often delays the opening of the ventures.

In spite of the cautious approach of the central government to retail joint ventures, all localities are reportedly very enthusiastic about them. Some provinces have trialled a number of cooperative retail ventures. Foreign-funded retail enterprises are estimated at 40–50 nationwide. Commercial enterprises seem to be very interested in undertaking joint ventures. Apart from importing advanced managerial expertise, they wish to share the import–export power enjoyed by joint ventures. At the time of writing (1996), over 100 commercial and materials-supply enterprises have been granted the right to import and export, including the First Department Store in Shanghai, the Wangfujing Department Store in Beijing, Beijing Xidan Bazaar and the People's Marketplace in Chengdu.

JOINT VENTURE CHAINSTORES

China's Ministry of Domestic Trade believes that conditions have become ripe for the country to develop chainstores. For the time being, development will focus on convenience chainstores, and experiments will be conducted with Chinese–foreign joint venture chainstores. In the past few years, chainstores have developed rapidly in China's open coastal cities and economically developed areas. To actively promote and support their development, the Ministry of Domestic Trade is drafting policies for their operation. As certain operational conditions must be met, including those involving production, consumption, transportation, telecommunications, and electronic processing, they can only be developed initially in China's large and medium-sized cities in coastal areas and developed areas.

The development of chainstores will focus on supermarkets, convenience stores, fast-food restaurants, and service outlets. To encourage the expansion of these stores, the central government and a number of local governments have adopted preferential policies toward tax and loans.

The Ministry of Domestic Trade is believed to be holding talks with some well-known foreign chainstore companies with a view to trialling Chinese–foreign joint venture chainstores. Informed sources say China will also try out other ways of cooperation. For example, foreign chainstore businesses may also run chainstores in China through contracting, leasing or management on a commission basis. Or foreign businesses may invest to build or co-manage material exchange and distribution centres for chainstores in China to provide advanced storage, transport and distribution facilities and equipment. Foreign businesses can also develop franchised operations in China and gradually establish a chainstore system.

Ministry Plans for Chainstores

The Ministry of Domestic Trade has drawn up a plan to develop chainstores on a trial basis in 35 big and medium-sized cities. Under the plan, China will have 6000 chainstores controlled by 300 parent enterprises with total annual sales of RMB 8 billion, or 5% of retail sales nationwide. Chainstores will multiply between 1996 and 2000. At the same time, the parent enterprises will grow into transregional corporations based on regional networks of chainstores. As of the year 2000, there will be 15,000 enterprises running 60,000 chainstores with total sales of RMB 120 billion, making up about 5% of the country's retail sales.

The plan focuses on the development of supermarkets and convenience stores. At the same time, chainstores will be developed in service trades such as fast food and laundering, as well as in small-scale services. The stores will be directly operated by the parent enterprises or linked up through franchises as is common practice internationally.

The stores will be mainly developed on a regional basis for the immediate future. The parent enterprises will be set up in city districts, provinces or in economic areas spanning several provinces like the Yangtze River Delta and the Pearl River Delta. Some parent enterprises operating nationally may also set up in trades such as gold, jewellery, wines and household electrical appliances.

China, at the time of writing (1996), boasts over 150 enterprises running over 2500 chainstores with annual sales of about RMB 3 billion. The stores can be divided into seven categories: supermarkets, community convenience stores, fine goods specialist, large department stores, supply stores, fast-food stores and service stores. State-owned department stores are now predominant, but those of other ownership are developing fast.

A major problem faced by transregional chainstores is local protectionism. Meanwhile, due to a shortage of funds and difficulties in obtaining loans, chainstores are on a smaller scale and clustered in small groups. A reliable supply of goods is difficult because of poor electronic communications facilities and transport facilities. Experts believe that these problems can be solved only by far-reaching economic reforms.

China has also repudiated the erstwhile diverse subsidy system in foreign trade and clearly stated that foreign traders have autonomy in management and assume sole responsibility for profits and losses. The State policy for encouraging the development of foreign trade will be implemented by adopting universal measures, for instance, by setting up special monetary bodies to promote foreign trade, foreign trade development funds and risk funds, and by export refunding.

Chainstores in Shanghai

Shanghai had, in 1996, more than 1500 chainstores chalking up sales totalling RMB 1.45 billion a year. This accounts for 1.9% of the city's total annual retail sales. There are now four kinds of chainstores in Shanghai.

(1) *Fast food chain stores*. After the debut of Kentucky Fried Chicken (KFC) in Shanghai in 1989, a number of big-name fast-food chainstores, including Huarong Fried Chicken, Xinya Fast Food and McDonald's, started operations in the city one after another leading to fierce competition between Chinese fast foods and Western snacks. Over the past five years, KFC has opened 10 restaurants in Shanghai achieving total sales of RMB 146 million in 1994—enough to launch five more restaurants.

(2) *Supermarket chains*. Construction of supermarkets started in Shanghai in 1991 and now there are a dozen supermarket chains in the city, such as Hualian, Lianhua, Baxian, Liannong, Zhonghui and Parkin. Last year, 133 supermarkets selling popular cheap foods, non-staple foods, vegetables and general merchandise opened for business, bringing the total number of supermarkets in the city to more than 400 with a corresponding growth in profits. The development of supermarkets in the city is among the fastest in the country.

(3) *Convenience shops*. These stores are mainly devoted to the retailing of minor commodities for the convenience of residents. There are nearly 1000 of them in Shanghai now, and they are growing in popularity. The development of such shops is also very rapid, exceeded only by that of supermarkets.

(4) *Specialty stores*. In the food industry, there are biscuit stores and bread stores such as the Sweet House, while in the fashion trade, there are chainstores selling garments under famous trademarks such as Crocodile.

CONCLUSION

Shanghai has been at the forefront of the booming retail industry in China. According to experts in Shanghai's commercial circles, the rise of chainstores in the city can be attributed to continued, rapid and healthy economic development and a big increase in the purchasing power of local residents. In 1995, Shanghai's gross domestic product (GDP) totalled RMB 190.67 billion, and its GDP per capita was close to that experienced in the initial stages of the development of chainstores overseas. Residents in Shanghai have also become used to buying new, quality products and services in a convenient way, and have accepted snacks, food in small packages and frozen foods—a good sign for the development of chainstores. It has been estimated that, by the end of 1996, another 100 popular large supermarkets and 300 convenience shops will have been built in Shanghai.

CHAPTER 13

NEGOTIATIONS, DISPUTES AND ARBITRATION

'Yes' in China may be the first word of agreement, but not always the last word in negotiations. 'Yes' is often simply another way of saying 'Let's begin talking seriously'. The Chinese often interpret the conclusion of a contract to mean that the two parties now understand each other well enough to begin asking further favours. What may be viewed as simply a favour to one side may seem like a costly concession to the other. For the Western party, a contract is a contract, and the obligations of the parties are those obligations spelled out in it. Western culture is goal-oriented: negotiations are simply a process through which the final goal—the contract—is reached.

Chinese society is process-oriented. Consequently, for the Chinese, negotiations often involve understandings and intentions not spelled out in the final contract. These can resurface at any time, often couched in phrases like, '...based on our friendship and mutual understanding, could you please...'. Because of Confucian values and the Chinese emphasis on interpersonal relations, these requests may have nothing to do with the contract terms at all, and range from things like, 'Can you get my kid into an American college to study?' to 'Our company/factory would like a new Mercedes Benz'.

CHINESE NEGOTIATION STYLES

Despite the emphasis on interpersonal relations, the Chinese are tough negotiators. Western businessmen often find contract negotiations in China to be a traumatic, stressful endurance test. Chinese negotiating tactics have been best described as being analogous to guerrilla warfare: 'Strike hard, retreat, seize a position, reject compromise, and strike again'.

The Chinese open negotiations by trying to establish their own ground rules. They do this by pressing their foreign counterparts to agree to certain general principles; the agreement to principles usually takes the form of a 'letter of intent'. To the Westerner, these principles may seem like ritual statements because they lack any kind of special detail.

Be careful—one should not make too many assumptions regarding initial formalities. The principles initially agreed to will set up a conceptual parameter within which the parties must work in order for discussions to progress. Later the Chinese may invoke these principles to suggest that the foreign party has not lived up to the spirit of 'mutual cooperation and benefit' initially agreed upon. The Chinese emphasis on general principles strikes an unusual chord in Western businessmen, since it contrasts sharply with the Western notion of focusing on details and hammering out specifics in the narrow context of a legal framework.

The Chinese like to dictate the pace of negotiations and the agenda. Little does the unwary Western businessman realise that real negotiating begins at the moment of arrival in China. In fact, the first-time visitor will feel he has been caught off-guard. On one visit a Western businessman may find his Chinese hosts waiting to greet him before he goes through Customs. On another visit the same businessman may have to wait outside in a milling airport crowd, until found by the representative of his host organisation. Even if the visitors take preparatory measures (such as booking their own hotels in advance), their Chinese hosts ultimately control the schedule. Controlling the other party's schedule gives the Chinese the element of surprise. Beware the visitor who arrives hot to hit the negotiating table: his hosts may have a few sightseeing tours (like a full-day drive to the Great Wall and back), followed by a heavy Peking Duck dinner in store for their jetlagged guest.

It is quite common for the Chinese to try to force reductions in the contract price in the last stages of discussion. Indeed, they will wait until the final touches are being put to negotiations—or at least appear to. That is when they set the stage for driving an even harder bargain. Once negotiations are over and everyone is getting ready to sign the contracts, foreign businessmen should try not to look too happy. The danger in doing so is that they might give the Chinese reason to suspect that they have been outdone in the agreement. One reason why the Chinese are not in a rush to make deals, according to some experts, is that they need to show their superiors what shrewd bargainers they are. 'It won't make them feel good if you conclude the deal in the shortest time', said one China trader. 'Go to see the Great Wall with them before beginning tough negotiations.'

DISPUTE RESOLUTION

Chinese culture places a premium on harmony; open conflict is something to be avoided. When disputes arise in a contract, the Chinese prefer to resolve them through amicable, non-binding conciliation talks between the parties. While such discussions will probably be frustrating, time-consuming and not entirely amicable, it is still the preferable means. In fact, most Chinese contracts contain a provision emphasising friendly negotiations in the event that disputes arise between the parties. The Foreign Economic Contract Law stipulates in Article 37 that: 'In the case of a dispute, contracting parties will do everything possible to settle it through consultation or mediation by a third party. If the parties do not want to settle their dispute through consultation or third-party mediation, or if the consultation or mediation fails, they may submit the case to Chinese or other arbitration bodies according to contract terms or a written agreement reached on arbitration after the dispute.'

Many contracts contain an arbitration clause designating arbitration in third countries in the event that friendly negotiations become less than friendly. The objective for the Chinese party is to avoid open confrontation, and (short of arbitration) keep the relationship going.

ARBITRATION LAW

After more than 40 years of experience in arbitration, China promulgated its first arbitration law on 31 August 1994; before, there were only regulations and decrees. The promulgation of the Arbitration Law not only established a unified arbitration system, but also enhanced the legal status of arbitration in China.

Most of the provisions of the Arbitration Law are in line with accepted principles of international arbitration and acceptable to the parties concerned who want to arbitrate in China under a familiar system. Contractual disputes between citizens of equal status, legal entities and other economic organisations, and disputes arising from property rights, may be put to arbitration. Disputes arising from marriage, adoption, guardianship, bringing up of children and inheritance or other issues which by law must be settled by administrative means, cannot be put to arbitration.

Before the Arbitration Law was passed, most arbitration was managed by administrative bodies. For example, the arbitration commission for economic contracts was established in the Administration of Industry and Commerce, and most of the arbitrators were officials of that Administration. Under the Arbitration Law, the arbitration commission is independent of the administrative bodies and supervises arbitration autonomously. Arbitration and litigation as a means of dispute resolution used to be very confusing. Parties were allowed to proceed with arbitration and litigation for the same dispute, or either party could appeal to the court against the award at any time. Under the Arbitration Law, once the parties agree to arbitration, they cannot bring a suit in the People's Court. The arbitration award is final and parties cannot appeal to the court unless certain situations stipulated in the Arbitration Law occur. Under the Arbitration Law, the parties to a dispute have the freedom to decide:

- to use arbitration or not;
- to appoint arbitrators;
- the place of arbitration;
- which arbitration commission is to be appointed;
- which issues are to be submitted to arbitration;
- what matters are to be recorded in the rulings; and
- whether the hearing is to be heard in an open court.

However, the parties are still not able to choose the arbitration rules and applicable law. Furthermore, the freedom of choosing arbitrators is limited because the parties can only choose arbitrators from the lists of arbitrators supplied by the arbitration commission.

Most foreigners prefer arbitration to litigation as a means of dispute settlement for the following reasons:

- the arbitral award can be enforced in the PRC since the PRC joined the New York Convention in 1986, while a judgment made by a foreign court may not be enforced by a Chinese court;
- the parties can appoint an arbitration tribunal of their own choice although they cannot select which Chinese court deals with the dispute; and because
- the parties can also agree to have the arbitration award made binding and final to avoid an appeal (often beneficial in commercial disputes).

Arbitration Agreements

An agreement to engage in arbitration to settle a dispute should first be reached by all parties concerned, expressing their free will and decision to accept arbitration. The agreement should include the arbitration clauses stipulated in the contracts, or other written agreements specifying the arbitration to be conducted before or after a dispute occurs, and must contain at least the following main points:

- the expression of intention by the parties to apply for arbitration;
- the matters to be brought for arbitration; and
- the arbitration commission and venue selected.

The effect of an agreement for arbitration stands independently and cannot be affected by the alteration, dissolution, termination or invalidity of the contract. If the parties concerned have doubts on the validity of an agreement for arbitration, a request can be made to the arbitration commission for a decision, or to the People's Court for a ruling, before the first hearing at the arbitration tribunal. If one party requests the arbitration commission to render a decision while the other party requests the People's Court for a ruling, the People's Court shall pass a ruling.

It is clearly stated in the Arbitration Law that the arbitration agreement must be reached with the free will of the parties. If there is no such agreement, the arbitration commission will refuse to accept the application for arbitration and the parties can apply for the cancellation of the arbitral award. Therefore, the Arbitration Law overrides those regulations which impose compulsory arbitration on parties when disputes arise.

In applying for arbitration, the parties concerned must submit the agreement and the application for arbitration to the arbitration commission which decides whether to accept them within five days of receipt. Before the new Arbitration Law was adopted, most of the arbitration authorities were under the State Administration of Industry and Commerce. Likewise, most of the arbitrators were appointed from among the Administration's officials. The arbitration commission is now theoretically independent and has autonomy in the supervision of arbitration.

The People's Court

Where the parties concerned have reached an agreement for arbitration, the People's Court will not accept a suit brought to the court by any one single party involved, except in cases where the agreement for arbitration is invalid.

When one party brings a suit before the People's Court without notifying the court that there is an agreement for arbitration and the other party submits the agreement for arbitration before the first hearing, the People's Court will reject the suit. If the other party fails to raise objections to the acceptance of the case by the People's Court before the first hearing, it is regarded as having submitted the agreement for arbitration and the People's Court continues the hearing.

Appointment of Arbitrators

An arbitration tribunal may consist of three arbitrators or just one; if the former, there should be a chief arbitrator. Where the parties concerned fail to decide on the composition of the arbitration tribunal or fail to choose arbitrators within the time-limit prescribed in the arbitration rules, the chairman of the arbitration commission makes the decision. An arbitrator must have or be:

- at least eight years' work experience in arbitration;
- at least eight years' experience as a lawyer;
- at least eight years' experience as a judge;
- engaged in law research and teaching, and in a suitable senior position; or
- legal knowledge and be engaged in professional work related to economics and trade, and in a suitable senior position or at an equivalent professional level.

The parties concerned have the right to request an arbitrator stand down if:

- the arbitrator is a party involved in the case or a blood relation or relative of the parties concerned or their attorneys;
- the arbitrator has vital personal interests in the case;
- the arbitrator has other relations with the parties or their attorneys involved in the case that might affect a fair ruling on the case; or if
- the arbitrator meets the parties concerned or their attorneys in private or has accepted gifts or attended banquets hosted by the parties concerned or their attorneys.

Arbitration is conducted independently according to the law, free from interference of administrative bodies, social groups or individuals. An arbitration tribunal has the right to establish the validity of a contract.

Arbitration Proceedings

After an arbitration commission has accepted an application, it delivers the arbitration rules and the list of the panel of arbitrators and other documents to the parties. Having received a copy of the application for arbitration, the respondent files a counter-claim with the arbitration commission which will then deliver the same to the claimant. If a respondent fails to submit a counter-claim, it will not affect the arbitration proceedings.

The arbitration tribunal may not hear a case in open session unless the parties concerned agree. If the tribunal deems it necessary to collect evidence, it may do so on its own initiative. The parties may question or substantiate the evidence and engage in debate during the hearing. At the end of the debate, the chief or sole arbitrator asks the parties for their final statement. The parties or their legal representatives may entrust lawyers or other attorneys to handle matters relating to arbitration.

Where evidence is sensitive, destroyed, missing, or hard to recover, or the arbitration award is hard to execute, the parties concerned may apply to place the disputed evidence or property under custody. Where a claimant has applied for custody of evidence or property, the arbitration commission must submit the application to the People's Court.

The arbitration tribunal may effect a reconciliation before making the arbitral award. Where an agreement is reached through reconciliation, the tribunal compiles the reconciliation document or makes an award based on the results of the agreement. The document of reconciliation and the arbitral award are equally binding legally.

Arbitral Awards

The arbitral award specifies the arbitration claims, facts in disputes, reasons for the award, result of the award, arbitration expenses and date of the award given, unless parties agree otherwise. The arbitration award is final: the arbitration commission or the People's Court will not accept a suit concerning the same dispute by any of the parties concerned.

The Arbitration Law provides for grounds on which the parties may apply for the cancellation of an arbitral award with the intermediate People's Court. An application for the cancellation of an arbitral award should be filed within six months of the date of receipt of the award. After the People's Court has accepted an application for the cancellation of an arbitral award and deems it necessary for the arbitration tribunal to make a new award, it must notify the tribunal to make a new ruling and order the termination of the cancellation. If the tribunal refuses to make a new ruling, the People's Court willl restore the cancellation. If the People's Court establishes that an arbitral award goes against the public interest, it will cancel it. It can also order the non-performance or cancellation of an award in accordance with law, and the parties in dispute may apply for arbitration pursuant to another agreement for arbitration newly reached by the parties, or bring a suit in the People's Court.

If one of the parties refuses to execute the award, the other party may apply for enforcement with the People's Court according to the relevant provisions of the Civil Procedure Law. The People's Court with which the application is filed should enforce it.

CONCLUSION

Negotiations, disputes and dispute resolution in China can be compared to sliding down a slippery ski slope. Sometimes the deterioration of relations leads to a gradual sliding down the hill even while one is trying to walk up. Generally speaking, the collapse of relationships begins when friendly discussions become acrimonious, leading to mediation. Arbitration is generally the last stage, when the relationship between the parties has become irreparably damaged. At this stage, one should try to get out of an investment situation, or resolve the situation in accordance with the procedures described in this chapter.

It is advisable to use negotiations and ongoing positive proactive efforts to maintain good relations with one's partner in either trade or investment in China.

PART 4

FINANCIAL ISSUES

CHAPTER 14

THE FINANCIAL SYSTEM

The restructuring of the banking system in China has been an important area of reform over the past five years in particular. In addition to dismantling the old State command economy system and creating a new system where market economics has become the key factor, the former State banks which once acted merely as branches of the People's Bank of China have now been transformed into commercial retail banks, with the People's Bank of China acting as the central monetary authority. This reform has been critical to the creation of a modern and international banking system in China.

In order to implement the Resolution of the Central Committee of the Chinese Communist Party concerning the establishment of a socialist market economy, the State Council promulgated:

- the Decision of the State Council on the Restructuring of the Banking System (the Decision) on 25 December 1993; and
- the Announcement of the People's Bank of China Concerning Further Reform of Foreign Exchange Control on 28 December 1993.

In 1994, these basic pieces of legislation began the country's restructuring of its banking system. The Decision points out that the aim of the restructuring is to establish, under the leadership of the State Council:

- a macro-regulatory and control system under the central bank which is independent in implementing monetary policy;
- a banking structure characterised by a separation of policy implementing banks from commercial banks;
- State-owned banks as the mainstay and coexisting with the numerous banking institutions; and
- a unified, open, orderly yet competitive monetary market system under strict administration.

TRANSFORMING THE PEOPLE'S BANK

The primary task is to transform the People's Bank of China into a central bank in the true sense of the word and establish it as a powerful macro-regulatory and control mechanism. Its principal functions are to:

- scientifically formulate and implement monetary policies and maintain a fundamental stability of the currency; and
- exercise strict surveillance over banking institutions to ensure a safe and effective operation of the banking system.

Powers and Responsibilities

The powers and responsibilities of the People's Bank of China and its branches at all levels are delineated as follows.

(1) The People's Bank of China has:
- the power to issue currency;
- the power to control basic currency supply and withdrawal; and
- the power to regulate the scale of loans and maintain administrative power over interest rates.

(2) The People's Bank of China branches from the provincial level down are in charge of:
- supervision and control of the money market;
- investigation;
- statistics and analysis;
- inter-bank short-term lending;
- the State coffers;
- cash allocations; and
- foreign exchange controls and inter-branch settlements.

Further Reform Policies

To further deepen the reform of the banking system, the People's Bank of China will exercise control over deposit reserve rates, central bank credit interest rates, central bank discount rates for foreign exchange operation and bill acceptance and public market operation business. Such measures will regulate the money supply and total social credit volume so as to maintain currency stability. Meanwhile, it is necessary to monitor the operations of commercial banks and establish a risk-prevention and control mechanism for credit capital.

Beginning in 1994, steps were taken gradually to control credit capital. The measures include a total volume control target, efforts to use the money supply volume, total credit volume, inter-bank short-term lending interest rates, bank payment reserve rates and other intermediate operational steps. These replace the traditional practice of the central bank's control of basic money supply and withdrawal through loans to commercial banks. Measures are aimed at encouraging re-discounts, doing public market business with State bonds and foreign exchange as the operational objects; exercising control in separating the policy implementing banks and commercial banks in their capital management and business operations, severing the direct connection between the basic money supply of the central bank from the issuing of loans for policy considerations, and exercising balance sheet ratio management and risk management over credit loans in Renminbi and foreign exchange to commercial banks.

COMMERCIALISING THE BANKING SYSTEM

To turn the State-owned specialised banks into truly commercial banks is a key link in restructuring the banking system. Policy implementing banks are to be established to remove policy-oriented business from specialised banks, and to reform existing specialised banks according to the general principles governing commercial banks.

Policy Banks

The policy implementing banks which have been established include the State Development Bank, the Import and Export Credit Bank of China and the Agricultural Development Bank of China. These banks are subject to the supervision of the People's Bank of China in their business operations; however, they are responsible for risks on their own, operate on a no-profit, no-loss basis and do not compete with commercial banks.

The State Development Bank handles credit loans and interest reduction business with regard to major State construction projects involving policy (including capital construction and technical transformation projects), and administers the People's Construction Bank of China and State investment institutions. The Import and

Export Credit Bank of China provides credit loans to buyers for the importation and to sellers for the exportation of complete plants of machinery and electrical equipment. The Agricultural Development Bank of China handles loans involving policy considerations for State-contracted purchases of grain, cotton and edible oil reserves and other farm products and by-products and for agricultural development projects, and acts as State agent in the allocation and supervision of funds to aid agriculture.

After the operations involving policy considerations have been taken away from State-owned specialised banks, the existing State-owned specialised banks (the Industrial and Commercial Bank of China, the Agricultural Bank of China, the Bank of China and the People's Construction Bank of China) will complete the switch over to State-owned commercial banks as quickly as possible. Their most fundamental features are independence in operation, liability for their own risks, profits and losses, and their autonomy.

Commercial Banks

The commercial banks in China include the State-owned commercial banks, the Bank of Communications, the CITIC Industrial Bank, the Guangda Bank, the Huaxia Bank, the China Merchants Commercial Bank, the Fujian Industrial Bank, the Guangdong Development Bank, the Shenzhen Development Bank, the Shanghai Pudong Development Bank and rural and urban cooperative banks.

Commercial banks are not allowed to invest in non-banking institutions, stocks or real estate. While observing the laws and regulations and professional standards of the banking industry, the banks may compete among themselves, with non-banking institutions and with Chinese-funded banks and foreign-funded banks either in or outside China.

Insurance, Trust, Finance and Securities Companies

Control over the insurance, securities, trust and banking industries is exercised separately. The State allows for appropriate development of various specialised insurance companies, trust and investment companies, securities companies, finance leasing companies, finance companies of enterprise groups and other non-banking institutions.

The restructuring of the insurance system should retain the separation of social insurance from commercial insurance, and the separation of government functions from enterprises. Trust and investment companies mainly handle trust loans and loans on behalf of clients, transactions in securities, financing and leasing, commission business and consultant business. The finance companies of enterprise groups mainly seek short-term loans by floating commercial instruments. Securities companies are not allowed to do business other than securities investment.

CREDIT FOR FOREIGN INVESTORS

The positive bank credit policies remain unchanged. At the same time, with the reform of the banking system, a money market will be established and perfected. For foreign-funded enterprises, an important channel for fundraising is to borrow from banks and other financial institutions. In accordance with:

- Article 3 of the Procedures for Loans by the Bank of China to Foreign-Funded Enterprises (the Procedures for Loans) promulgated by the Bank of China on 24 April 1987;
- Article 78 of the Regulations for the Implementation of the Law of the People's Republic of China on Chinese–Foreign Joint Ventures;
- Article 17 of the Law on Chinese–Foreign Cooperative Enterprises;
- the Regulations for the Administration of Foreign Banking Institutions in the People's Republic of China promulgated by the State Council on 25 February 1994;
- the Provisions for the Administration of Security provided by Domestic Institutions for Foreign Institutions approved by the People's Bank of China on 1 August 1991;
- the Interim Provisions for the Statistics and Monitoring of Foreign Debts; and
- the Rules for the Implementation of Registration of Foreign Debts and relevant provisions,

foreign-invested enterprises may, in light of their business requirements, take loans from the Bank of China or other domestic banks or banking institutions approved by the People's Bank of China, or borrow in foreign exchange directly from foreign banks, international banking institutions, foreign-funded banks in China, Chinese–foreign joint banks, or foreign-funded or Chinese–foreign non-banking institutions (foreign-funded banking institutions). However, the latter must register transactions with the State Administration of Exchange Control or its branches mainly to enable it to record and monitor forex movements.

BORROWING FROM DOMESTIC BANKING INSTITUTIONS

In accordance with the provisions of Article 4 of the Procedures for Loans, the Bank of China may sign loan agreements with a foreign-invested enterprise. The Bank of China aims to build up its credit management. Article 5 of the Procedures for Loans provides that the Bank of China may do the following credit business with foreign-invested enterprises.

Loans for Fixed Assets

These are loans to be used for construction, technology and the purchase and installation of equipment for projects involving capital construction and technical upgrading. There are four forms:

- medium and short-term loans;
- credit on the part of the buyer;
- banking group loans; and
- project loans.

Loans for Working Capital

These are loans to be used to fund an enterprise engaged in commodity production and distribution and other normal business activities. There are three forms:

- loans for production and operation;
- temporary loans; and
- overdrafts on active accounts.

Loans against Spot Exchange

Loans in this category are issued according to the provisions of the Interim Provisions for Loans in Renminbi to Foreign-Funded Enterprises against Foreign Exchange promulgated by the Bank of China on 12 December 1986. Loans in Renminbi against foreign exchange refers to a loan in Renminbi for which a foreign-funded enterprise applies to the Bank of China by using as collateral the foreign exchange it has or loans from outside China.

The loan cannot be repaid before it is due. When the loan is due, it should be repaid in the original amount of Renminbi and the Bank of China will return the original amount of foreign exchange without regard to fluctuations in the exchange rate. In the event of failure to repay the Renminbi loan, the foreign exchange will be taken by the bank as security.

A Renminbi loan issued by the bank to a foreign-funded enterprise cannot exceed the value of the foreign exchange used by the borrower as collateral at the exchange rate against Renminbi (the buying price) published by the Bank of China on the day of the issue of the loan. The Renminbi loan provided by the bank and the foreign exchange placed by a joint venture as security are provided interest-free.

Loans for Reserve

These are special loans that a foreign-funded enterprise applies for. Applications are examined and approved by the People's Bank of China. The loans may be in Renminbi or in foreign exchange, including the US dollar, the Japanese yen, the Hong Kong dollar, the German mark and other convertible currencies approved by the Bank of China.

CONDITIONS AND GUARANTEES FOR LOANS

According to the provisions of Article 7 of the Procedures for Loans, a foreign-funded enterprise applying for a loan should meet the following prerequisites.

(1) It should possess a business licence issued by the Chinese administration for industry and commerce and an account opened with the Bank of China.

(2) The registered capital of the enterprise must be contributed on time and verified in accordance with the law.

(3) The decision has been made by the board of directors to request the loan and a letter of authorisation submitted.

(4) The enterprise's fixed asset projects to be financed already approved by the planning authorities.

(5) The ability of the enterprise to repay the loan and to furnish a guarantee for the repayment of the principal and interest.

When a foreign-invested enterprise applies to the Bank of China for a loan and the latter requires the applicant to provide a guarantee, the applicant must provide a recognised guarantee. In accordance with Article 16 of the Procedures for Loans, a foreign-invested enterprise may submit to the Bank of China an irrevocable letter of guarantee provided by a credit-worthy and loan-worthy banking institution, enterprise or other unit. Alternatively, the enterprise may mortgage to the Bank of China its assets and rights as collateral security for the principal and interest on a loan. Assets and rights which may be mortgaged may be:

- buildings and machinery and equipment;
- marketable commodities in stock;
- deposits or deposit receipts;
- convertible securities and bills; or
- stock equities and other transferable rights.

The enterprise must sign a mortgage contract with the Bank of China for a loan against collateral and the mortgage document must be notarised by a Chinese public notary. The collateral must be fully insured with the People's Insurance Corporation of China. When the Bank of China deems it necessary, a foreign-invested enterprise must provide both credit and mortgage.

Terms of a Loan

The Procedures for Loans state that the term of a loan to a foreign-invested enterprise begins on the day the loan agreement comes into effect and terminates on the day that repayment of the principal and interest and fees fall due.

The term for a loan on a fixed asset item cannot exceed seven years; the term for special projects may be extended appropriately with the approval of the Bank of China but the extension cannot exceed 12 months. The term for a loan to be used as working capital cannot exceed 12 months. The term for loans against collateral vary in line with different categories of loans: short-term loans against collateral may be for three months, six months or a year; the term for a medium-term loan against collateral may be longer than one year but may not exceed five years.

Interest Rates

The Bank of China fixes its rate of interest for loans to foreign-invested enterprises at the interest rate for loans to State-owned enterprises. The interest rates on loans in foreign exchange are fixed in accordance with the comprehensive interest rates set by the central office of the Bank of China, or set through consultation by both parties in accordance with interest rates on the international market. The interest rates for using buyer's credit or other credits are fixed on the basis of the contract plus the interest differences.

Procedures for Loans

Loans are processed in two steps in accordance with Article 13 of the Procedures for Loans. First, a foreign-invested enterprise submits to the Bank of China an application for a loan together with relevant certificates and other information as is required for a specific loan. Usually included are the project proposal of the foreign-invested enterprise, a feasibility report, contracts, articles of association, business licence, relevant financial plans, production and marketing contracts and a written letter of undertaking; in the event of a loan for a construction project, the project proposal and construction order, and relevant documents are required.

Second, the Bank of China examines and assesses the loan application and relevant certificates and information submitted. Upon approval of the application, the creditor and borrower sign a loan agreement.

In the event of a credit loan, the loan agreement is attached as an appendix with a loan guarantee provided by a guarantor enterprise approved by the Bank of China. In the event of a loan against collateral, the loan agreement is attached as an appendix with mortgage documents signed by the borrower enterprise and confirmed by the Bank of China. In the event of a loan in Renminbi with foreign exchange as mortgage, the procedure defined in the Interim Procedures for Loans in Renminbi to Foreign-Invested Enterprises against Mortgage will be followed.

Defaulting on a Loan

In accordance with Articles 18, 20 and 21 of the Procedure for Loans, a foreign-invested enterprise must repay the loan and pay all the interest and fees on time. If an enterprise fails to abide by the provisions of the loan agreement, the Bank of China has the right to take the following remedies. It can:

- order it to make corrections within a specified time;
- suspend the issue of the loan;
- retrieve the loan ahead of schedule; or
- notify the guarantor to perform its obligations.

If a foreign-invested enterprise defaults, the enterprise (or unit) which provided the letter of guarantee is responsible for paying the principal and interest on the loan; in the event of a loan against a mortgage, the Bank of China has priority in retrieving the principal and interest on the loan and other arrears. A surcharge of 20% to 50% of interest on the arrears of a loan due is generally applied.

FOREIGN EXCHANGE LOANS FROM FOREIGN-FUNDED BANKING INSTITUTIONS

A foreign-invested enterprise in China may borrow from a foreign bank, an international banking institution or other foreign-funded banking institutions. However, such a loan must be based on a proper settlement of the guarantee in foreign exchange.

In accordance with the Procedure for Providing Foreign Exchange Guarantee by an Institution within the Territory of the People's Republic of China which was approved by the People's Bank of China on 1 August 1991, a foreign exchange guarantee refers to a pledge an institution makes on the foreign exchange capital it possesses to a creditor outside China or a foreign-funded bank, or a Chinese–foreign joint bank, or a foreign-funded or Chinese–foreign joint non-banking institution in China.

When the debtor fails to clear its debts in foreign exchange in pursuance of the loan agreement, the guarantor may discharge its obligations in foreign exchange. Institutions and units allowed to provide foreign exchange guarantees are limited to those banking institutions licensed to do foreign exchange guarantee business and to those non-banking corporate bodies that have foreign exchange income.

CONCLUSION

Many foreign banks and insurance companies as well as other financial institutions are now interested in establishing a branch in China. It is the intention of the Chinese government to first establish a secure and sound financial and banking system for domestic entities before opening this market to foreign participation on a large scale.

Nevertheless, a number of foreign banks and financial institutions have been licensed to establish branches in China. It is expected that these permissions will increase over the coming years as the general internationalisation of the banking system in China proceeds.

CHAPTER 15

FOREIGN EXCHANGE

China's currency, the Renminbi, has for years been a non-convertible currency. This has been a major problem for foreign investors investing in China and looking for a way to repatriate profits.

China's road toward convertibility has involved a number of important reforms which have been implemented in a step-by-step manner. This chapter presents an overview of these reforms, and examines how foreign investors can resolve their foreign exchange problems in China in a practical manner.

EARLY POLICIES

During the years following Liberation in 1949, China embarked on a policy of economic centralisation, concentrating on domestic economic issues except where international support for brother socialist countries was required. Because China's external relations were rather limited prior to 1979, foreign exchange inflow and outflow were also very limited, and there was no need for legislation governing foreign exchange.

When the Eleventh National People's Congress decided in 1978 to implement a new policy emphasising economic development and a role for foreign investment in a more open economy, the need for legislation to address foreign exchange issues became immediate and pressing. In 1980, the first legislation concerning foreign exchange was promulgated by the State Council, the Provisional Regulations for Exchange Control of the People's Republic of China. The effect of this legislation was to address fundamental issues concerning foreign exchange, thereby implementing central government policy decisions. Some of the more important provisions were the following.

(1) The establishment of the State Administration of Exchange Control under the People's Bank of China as the general authority in China responsible for handling and implementing all matters relating to foreign exchange control.

(2) Permission for only financial institutions and banks which have received proper government authorisation to engage in foreign exchange activities (at the time, only the Bank of China was permitted though, in time, permission would be eventually granted to a wider range of institutions).

(3) The establishment of the foreign exchange retention system for all enterprises in China. Under this system, domestic enterprises were able to retain a certain percentage of foreign exchange from their domestic exchange earnings.

REFORMS TO THE FOREIGN EXCHANGE SYSTEM

Since the Renminbi is not convertible into foreign exchange, foreign investment enterprises need to generate enough foreign exchange from their business activities to cover their own foreign exchange expenditures (such as imports) and allow them enough foreign exchange to remit profits abroad.

The long-term goal of China's reforms of the foreign exchange system is to make Renminbi conditionally and then eventually convertible. The reforms have so far implemented a unified and managed floating exchange rate which applies to all settlements and transactions of foreign exchange on the basis of demand and supply in the market. The measures involved in the reforms include the following:

(1) the abolition of the old foreign exchange retention and turning-over system in order to set up an exchange settlement and concentration system;

(2) the abolition of authorisation procedures to allocate foreign exchange according to normal external payment items under the current account, and the implementation of a system to purchase foreign exchange from banks and make the Renminbi conditionally convertible under the current account;

(3) the establishment of a national unified inter-bank foreign exchange market, and an improved mechanism to determine the exchange rate;

(4) better management of the system of cancellation after verification of foreign exchange payments and receipts;

(5) reinforcement of external debts administration and control drains of domestic capital; and

(6) the establishment of an international payment and receipts registration system.

On 1 January 1994, China unified the former dual Renminbi exchange rates. The exchange settlement and concentration system was officially implemented on 1 April 1994; China's Foreign Exchange Trading System Center officially opened on 18 April 1994. The reforms have already achieved a substantial breakthrough. One of the key reforms was to implement a system of selling the foreign exchange receipts of all domestic enterprises, public institutions, government agencies and social organisations in China. Foreign exchange earnings which fell into the following categories (except those of foreign investment enterprises) were all sold off to the designated foreign exchange banks for Renminbi based on the exchange rates listed by the banks:

(1) foreign exchange earnings from exports, transit trade and other trading activities;

(2) foreign exchange earnings from services provided by communication and transportation, post and telecommunications, insurance, and other service industries, and from inter-governmental transfer; and

(3) net foreign exchange proceeds from foreign exchange operations of the banks which are required to be turned over to the State, and foreign exchange returns from investments abroad which are subject to repatriation.

Other foreign exchange receipts were also required to be sold off to banks. Foreign exchange earnings in the following categories were permitted to be held in foreign exchange in accounts opened with designated foreign exchange banks:

(1) foreign exchange remittances to China for the purpose of investment by non-resident legal entities or individuals;

(2) foreign exchange received from external borrowing, and debt or equity issuance;

(3) funds remitted back to China by service contract companies during the contract period of their overseas projects;

(4) receipts from foreign donations and grants approved for specific purposes;

(5) foreign exchange receipts of diplomatic missions and offices of international organisations and other non-resident legal entities in China; and

(6) foreign exchange held by individuals.

Foreign Exchange Payments

After introducing the system of purchasing foreign exchange from the banks, the existing authorisation procedure of allocating foreign exchange according to the State plan for normal external payment items under the current account was abolished. Foreign exchange needed by domestic enterprises, public institutions, government agencies and social organisations for external payments under current accounts is now paid in Renminbi, upon presentation of the following documentation:

(1) import quotas, licences or other authorisation to import issued by the departments concerned, and the relevant import contract for those items subject to import quotas or import restrictions;

(2) registration verification and the relevant contract to import those items subject to import voluntary registration;

(3) contracts to import and notification for payment from overseas financial institutions for all other imported items other than those in the above two categories, which are in conformity with State regulations; and

(4) payment agreements or contracts, and notification for payment from overseas financial and non-financial institutions for commercial payment under the non-trade account.

Foreign exchange purchases

Purchase of foreign exchange for non-commercial payments or for withdrawal of foreign currency in cash must be in accordance with the relevant regulations on financial and foreign exchange control. The authorisation procedures continue to be in effect for foreign exchange remittances for overseas investment, lending and donations.

After the introduction of the systems for selling and buying foreign exchange at the banks, a national unified inter-bank foreign exchange market was established. The designated foreign exchange banks are the main participants in the inter-bank market; their main functions are to facilitate the matching of long and short foreign exchange positions of the different designated banks, and to provide clearing and settlement services for banks.

RATES

The People's Bank of China publishes daily the median rate of

Renminbi against US dollars according to the transaction price prevailing in the inter-bank foreign exchange market the previous day. It also, with reference to the international foreign exchange market, publishes the Renminbi rate against other major foreign currencies.

Based on the foreign exchange rates published by the People's Bank, the designated banks will then list their own exchange rates within the floating range designated by the People's Bank, and purchase or sell foreign exchange to their customers at the listed rates. With the aim of stabilising the domestic currency, the listed exchange rates of different banks are basically compatible and relatively stable through inter-bank foreign exchange trading and the intervention of the People's Bank through buying and selling of foreign exchange in the foreign exchange market.

CONTROL OF FOREX BY FOREIGN INVESTORS

Newly established companies with foreign investment, whether they be joint ventures or wholly foreign-owned, must undertake foreign exchange management operations. They can still keep their foreign exchange accounts with either the designated foreign exchange banks or foreign banks in China. If the external payments of these enterprises are within the scope authorised by State regulations, (that is, to service the foreign exchange debts incurred with domestic financial institutions), they may make the payments directly from the outstanding balances of their foreign exchange accounts.

After review and approval by the State foreign exchange administrative departments, such enterprises may purchase foreign exchange from the designated banks for the purposes of production, operation, debt service, and profit and dividend remittance. This facility is not enjoyed by domestic enterprises. In addition, the unification of China's dual Renminbi exchange rates benefits the foreign investment environment. The advantages lie with the following.

(1) As the foreign exchange ratio is higher than the former foreign exchange rate quotation following the unification of the dual exchange rate, foreign investors' ratio of capital contribution converted at the exchange ratio is more than that of the previous exchange rate quotation. Moreover, it can solve the contradiction between converting the registered capital at the exchange rate quotation and calculating the outward bonus at the market swap rate.

(2) The unification of the dual Renminbi exchange rates, the inter-bank foreign exchange market and prohibition on foreign currency circulation in China benefits a national unified foreign exchange market and stabilises the exchange rate.

Balancing Forex

Foreign investment enterprises are required in principle to maintain a balance between payments and receipts. If foreign exchange payments and revenues are unbalanced, enterprises should solve the problem through enhancing their forex earnings or increasing the export ratio. In order to absorb more foreign investment, China maintains that foreign investment enterprises must keep their balance of foreign exchange through expanding exports. China also maintains the 'using the market in exchange for technology' policy to give foreign investment enterprises appropriate access to the domestic market and, the same time, adopts flexible measures to help foreign investors keep the balance of foreign exchange.

Regulations on Balancing Forex

In 1986, in a move to address these critical investor concerns, the State Council promulgated the Regulations Concerning the Balance of Foreign Exchange Income and Expenditures by Chinese–Foreign Equity Joint Ventures (the Balancing Regulations), which were later altered so as to apply to all three types of foreign investment enterprise in China (equity joint ventures, cooperative joint ventures, and wholly foreign-owned enterprises).

Foreign investors with imbalanced foreign exchange receipts and disbursement can use their Renminbi profits to reinvest in domestic enterprises and bring out new foreign exchange or increase their foreign exchange earnings. They can earn foreign exchange through newly increased foreign exchange earnings from their reinvestment enterprises—remitting their lawful profit as well as enjoying the preferential treatment of the refund as part of the income tax already paid. Those who reinvest with Renminbi can enjoy the same treatment as investments with foreign exchange. Domestic enterprises with foreign stock equity of over 25%, and which receive foreign investment in Renminbi, are regarded as foreign investment enterprises and can enjoy the treatment accorded to foreign investment enterprises.

On 29 January 1996, the Regulations for Foreign Exchange of the

Republic of China were promulgated by the State Council. These regulations allow China to adopt over-the-counter trading of currencies through the banking system, and formalise the foreign exchange trading system now operated largely through the inter-bank market in Shanghai. These regulations are expected to allow a more flexible system then previously imagined and form a sound basis for convertibility.

FROM SWAP CENTRE TO INTER-BANK MARKET

By 1993, there were over 100 foreign exchange Swap Centres throughout the country, of which 18 became 'open markets' where daily trading took place. These were established as an interim solution and were in the form of brokerages operated by local branches of the State Administration of Foreign Exchange Control. The centres became a very important part of the Chinese economy, establishing a market system value for trading foreign exchange and Renminbi between foreign investment enterprises as well as domestic enterprises.

On 1 January 1994, the Chinese Government removed the official State peg on the Renminbi's rate and floated it to reflect its market value (as determined by a national average of the various Swap Centre rates throughout the country). On 28 March 1994, new regulations were issued which disallowed participation at the Swap Centres by domestic enterprises. The use of foreign exchange to pay for products of foreign investment enterprises on the local market was also banned.

In a move to further consolidate China's foreign exchange system, and to systematise the Renminbi exchange rate, the China Foreign Exchange Trading System (CFETS), China's first inter-bank market, was established in Shanghai on 18 April 1994. Instituting a membership system, the CFETS administers and supervises the trading at its branches established in the following cities: Shanghai, Beijing, Tianjin, Guangzhou, Shenzhen, Xiamen, Wuhan, Qingdao, Changsha, Nanjing, Chengdu and Hangzhou.

All foreign exchange trading between financial institutions in China must now be carried out through the CFETS. In 1996, some Swap Centres remain as interim solutions for foreign investment enterprises.

RENMINBI CONVERTIBILITY

Renminbi convertibility is certainly on the cards for the future. Such planning is consistent with China's policy goals in respect of increasing inward foreign investment and expanding international trade. The speed with which China moves towards convertibility will, to a large extent, depend on such critical factors as its ability to:

- control inflation;
- retain an overall trade surplus;
- maintain a consistently high level of foreign exchange reserves; and
- continue its successful policy of monetary intervention within the context of a transitional economy seeking to achieve a natural balance between State planning and market orientation.

RECENT AND FUTURE MEASURES

Measures introduced between 1993 and 1996 to streamline China's foreign exchange system have included the following.

(1) The unification of the variable market rates at which the Renminbi is traded at foreign exchange adjustment centres (Swap Centres) throughout China.

(2) The official floating of the Renminbi rate based on a national market average (first based on the various Swap Centre rates, and later on the current CFETS trading rate).

(3) The phasing out of the Foreign Exchange Certificate as an interim currency used by foreign visitors and representative offices.

(4) The creation of the China Foreign Exchange Trading System, and the inter-bank swap market in Shanghai, to be followed by the phasing out of the Swap Centres.

(5) The recent creation of regional inter-bank swap markets under the China Foreign Trading System inter-bank market.

(6) The introduction of the over-the-counter trading at the commercial banks.

(7) Preparation for the introduction of a foreign exchange futures market.

CONCLUSION

China is clearly moving towards a system of free convertibility. Statements made on several occasions in 1996 by Vice Premier Zhu Rongji and the People's Bank of China have indicated that convertibility will most likely be achieved in 1997. This will be a major step providing a foundation for China's entry into the international trading community: China's entry into GATT will leave bilateral trade conflicts behind. Thus China will be poised to ascend to the position of the world's foremost export-oriented economy, thereby achieving economic superpower status.

CHAPTER 16
EMERGING SECURITIES MARKETS

When the concept of establishing securities markets in China was first discussed openly, Western observers could not believe the possibility of China developing successful securities exchanges in the near future. Thus it surprised many when, in 1990, China opened its first securities markets in Shanghai and Shenzhen. Soon B shares were being issued for foreign exchange to overseas investors in addition to the domestic A shares.

The securities markets have been the driving force behind new development and corporate restructuring in China, with State-owned enterprises becoming shareholding companies listed on the exchanges. Legislation covers all aspects of securities trading, and a securities regulatory authority has been established to oversee activities. This chapter describes the development of the securities markets in China and the structure of the regulatory framework.

THE DEVELOPMENT OF CHINA'S SECURITIES MARKETS

At a time when State planning still dominates economic policy, the Chinese Government has been breaking new ground by giving formal recognition to the establishment of securities trading floors, the very epitome of a market-driven economy.

A high-level body, the China Securities Regulation Commission, has recently been established to oversee the developing securities industry in China. In 1992, the Asian Development Bank granted US$600,000 through the People's Bank of China to be used for the development of China's securities markets.

For a number of years, the securities industry in China concentrated only on bond trading. Then, on 27 November 1990, the People's Government of Shanghai Municipality promulgated new Regulations of Shanghai Municipality on the Management of Securities Trading. The promulgation of these regulations was timed to follow the opening of the Pudong new area, a move by the central government aimed at restoring Shanghai's former glory as the financial centre of China. Ironically, the promulgation of similar measures in Shenzhen was delayed so as to allow for the formal establishment of the Shanghai Exchange, despite the existence of already active trading on the Shenzhen Exchange.

In 1986, bond trading re-emerged in major coastal cities such as Shanghai, Tianjin, Beijing, Shenyang, Harbin and Guangzhou. These cities individually established their own markets for the trading of bonds. Since that time, bond trading has grown throughout the country, with trading volumes averaging 200 million yuan a month in 1996. This staggering volume is not so surprising in light of the increase in domestic savings since 1989. The Chinese population had, in 1996, an estimated purchasing power of 912.3 billion yuan.

Two key regulations were promulgated to establish a framework under which China's bond markets could operate and through which bonds could be issued. The Regulations on the Administration of Enterprise Bonds established a basic framework for regulating the trading of bonds and also established procedures to allow State-owned enterprises to issue bonds in order to mobilise capital. When Chinese firms sought to mobilise foreign exchange through the issue of bonds abroad, the Regulations on the Control of Bonds Issued Abroad by Domestic Institutions were promulgated so that such issues could be carried out legally. The Control Regulations established a number of procedures by which institutions could apply to issue bonds in foreign jurisdictions. At the same time, they also established certain requirements which these institutions had to meet in order to issue international bonds. In addition, the regulations provided the mechanism to control the use of funds raised from such bond issues.

Two key organisations in China are responsible for the supervision of the bond markets: the State Administration of Exchange Control and the Securities Trading Automated Quotation System. The State Administration of Exchange Control, a bureau established directly under the People's Bank of China, is responsible for coordinating and supervising international bond issues. Its key role is to supervise the repayment of funds which might involve foreign exchange. The Securities Trading Automated Quotation System was established as a national market network system. As a service, it links up domestic securities firms, trust and investment companies, and provides a network between the different regions in which these companies are established. It also facilitates transactions between its member companies, providing services which include centralised clearance, settlement and price quotations.

EXISTING STOCK-MARKETS

There are only two securities exchanges in China permitted to actually trade company shares. Both the Shanghai and the Shenzhen Securities Exchanges were established in late 1990 by the People's Bank of China and operate under the supervision of the local branch of the China Securities Regulation Commission. When stock trading formally commenced on 19 December 1990 in Shanghai, Shenzhen had already jumped the gun by trading on 1 December. Despite the greater volume of activity on the Shenzhen exchange, the central government authorities have been giving greater support and emphasis to the development of the Shanghai exchange, as part of a general effort to promote the once-dynamic city as China's future financial centre over the free-wheeling and entrepreneurial Special Economic Zone of the South. In both markets only spot trading is allowed. When customers enter the market either to buy or sell securities, they must entrust a member; entrustment may be through personal contact or by telephone, telegraph, telex, fax or even a written letter.

There are two main regulations, one governing each market. The Regulations of Shanghai Municipality on the Management of Securities Trading establish application procedures for dealers to trade on the exchange. The regulations also cover the issuance, circulation and trading of securities in the Shanghai Administrative Area. Similarly, the Shenzhen Provisional Measures Controlling the Issue and Trading of Securities also establish listing and dealing requirements. The Shenzhen Measures, like the Shanghai Regulations, provide for the regulation of share trading and issues on the Shenzhen Municipal Exchange. Both pieces of legislation provide for the establishment of local supervisory boards. The Shanghai Regulations establish the Securities and Trade Association of Shanghai, while the Shenzhen Measures set out the responsibilities of the Shenzhen Securities Exchange.

Both are similar in nature, leaving one to suspect that one body of legislation was largely borrowed from the other. Consequently, a basic pattern of securities legislation may be expected in other exchanges developing throughout the country. The central government is expected to draft comprehensive national legislation in the future.

In both pieces of legislation, the issuance of securities is subject to approval from local authorities, namely the local branch of the People's Bank of China. Sources have observed, however, that although formal power to grant approval lies with the local People's

Bank in each city, final decisions on most key issues are still being made in Beijing—the central government wishes to maintain a close watch on the development of both markets.

The current securities legislation does not address the issue of foreign participation: it does not necessarily allow for foreign participation, nor does it specifically exclude it either. In this regard, China has already expanded the scope of listed stocks on the exchanges to include foreign joint venture enterprises. B Shares are also issued for sale to foreign nationals and foreign securities companies. These shares are denominated in Renminbi, but sold for foreign exchange.

Despite some hurdles and restraints, overwhelming emphasis is being placed on reviving Shanghai's former status as the financial centre of China. It appears that, for the time being, the development of securities markets will be limited to Shanghai and Shenzhen as experimental grounds. Nevertheless, it is understood that Tianjin, Wuhan and other cities have their own plans to develop markets. While approval from the central government is unlikely in the near future, there is always the possibility of unofficial trading taking place.

DEVELOPMENT OF THE SHAREHOLDING SYSTEM

China began to experiment with the shareholding system in Shanghai in 1984. Initially, 11 enterprises were transformed, one after another, into shareholding enterprises. Rather than call the exercise a 'privatisation' which has slight political overtones, the term *gufenhua* or 'shareholding transformation' was employed. By 1990, the central government had determined that both Shanghai and Shenzhen were to establish stock exchanges.

In 1996, China's stock exchanges are limited only to these two cities as experimental markets. There was an attempt earlier this year by Hainan Province to establish its own stock-market. This, however, was stopped when Zhu Rongji, the Vice Premier, visited Hainan and ordered, on behalf of the central government, that the market be closed. The experiment in issuing shares has become for the central government an important vehicle through which capital may be raised 'for socialist development'. At first, only Chinese citizens could trade stocks in Shenzhen and Shanghai; China's foreign exchange controls made it almost impossible for foreign investors to participate.

B Share Issue

In 1992, in a bold new move, China permitted the issuing of B shares to foreign investors. These shares are quoted in Renminbi but sold for foreign exchange and may be purchased through Chinese brokers.

They are traded in non scrip form. After the registration and transfer of ownership has been done by computer, a shareholder will be issued a voucher as evidence of holding stocks. Vouchers cannot be used for circulation or mortgaging purposes. They include the following information:

- stock account number;
- name of individual or organisation holding the stock;
- the name of the stock;
- the amount of stocks being dealt in;
- the date of registration; and
- other details as required.

Dividend interest and other legal income from B shares are valued in Renminbi and paid in foreign currency. Foreign investors must be aware, however, that they are required to pay taxes in accordance with Chinese regulations in respect of all dividends, bonuses and income derived from B share transactions. After taxation, however, because the B shares are originally paid for in foreign exchange, the profits derived from the purchase and sale of B shares may be remitted from China. Holders of B shares may also remit funds assigned them following the liquidation of the company.

B share issues are targeted primarily at foreign securities firms and investment institutions establishing funds to invest in China's markets. Given the small number of firms that are currently trading, and the even smaller number presently listing B shares, foreign merchant bankers are scrambling to obtain underwriting business. These merchant banks are in turn establishing China funds to invest in what has the potential to become the largest securities market in the world. So far, these funds have been oriented towards 'greater China', investing in securities listed in both Taiwan and Hong Kong in order to spread their risks while placing a small percentage of their investment in B shares.

Authorities Governing the Issue of B shares

The first legislation concerning the issue of B shares was promulgated on 22 November 1991 by the People's Bank of China and the Shanghai

Municipal People's Government—the Shanghai Municipality Administration of Special Renminbi Shares Procedures. These procedures gave general authority to the People's Bank of China in the Shanghai Municipality, in collaboration with the State Administration of Foreign Exchange Control of Shanghai, to authorise and oversee the issue and trading of B shares; the Shanghai State Administration has responsibility for the day-to-day administration and supervision of B shares. The procedures also set out the guidelines for brokers to engage in the issue and trading of B shares, and the rights and obligations of shareholders in this regard.

The Shanghai Procedures were followed only a few days later, on 25 November 1991, by the Shanghai Municipality Implementing Rules for the Administration of Special Renminbi Share Procedures, promulgated by the People's Bank of China's Shanghai Branch. These Rules provided more details in respect of the opening of trading accounts, the trading of shares, and the rules governing financial institutions in the issue and trading of B shares. Supplementary Rules on the Trading Business of Special Renminbi Shares of the Shanghai Securities Exchange were promulgated on 18 February 1992 by the Shanghai Securities Exchange itself. These rules provided for the registration of investors and the opening of special accounts to trade in B shares, and trading procedure details.

The Interim Procedures under Control of Shenzhen Special B Type Renminbi Stocks were promulgated by the People's Bank of China and the Shenzhen People's Government on 5 December 1991. These procedures provided for the issue and trading of B shares, providing particular details in respect of foreign exchange. The Shenzhen Interim Procedures were followed, on 29 January 1992, by the Provisional Rules on the Registration of Shenzhen Special B Type Renminbi Stocks, which stated that B Shares are on par with common stocks of Renminbi par value in rights and obligations. The key difference between shares and ordinary Renminbi stocks is that the B shares are sold for foreign currency. The Registration Rules also provide details of the issue of bonuses and dividends.

Shenzhen Interim Procedures

According to the Shenzhen Interim Procedures, the People's Bank of China is the authority responsible for governing B shares. The local People's Bank in Shenzhen is, in theory, the governing authority in collaboration with the local State Administration of Exchange Control. The authority granted to these two organisations includes:

- the power to formulate and revise regulations concerning B shares trading;
- the power to approve issues listed; and
- the power to approve those institutions permitted to act for agents in the transaction of B shares.

Together, these two institutions may examine the finances of companies issuing B shares and supervise all foreign exchange entering the market. Although, in theory, decisions are made at a local level, many observers of the developing markets say most decisions in respect of B share issues are still very much influenced by Beijing.

In order to establish a B share listing in Shenzhen, the company issuing the shares must prove that it has substantial foreign exchange income. Furthermore, the company must be approved as a 'joint stock company' which has limited liability. It must have articles of association approved by the government, and undergo an Assets Evaluation Report by an assets evaluation institution certified by a public accounting firm. Any evaluation of State-owned assets must be confirmed in writing from the State. Such an evaluation should include a profit and loss account for at least three years, certified by a public accounting firm.

The issue of B shares must be entrusted to an institution which has been granted special permission to engage in securities business; it must have the approval of the People's Bank of China. It may, in turn, organise overseas securities firms to participate in the underwriting and brokerage of B shares. Any institution given permission to issue and deal in B shares must open a special account at a bank in China designated by the authorities. All funds raised from the issue of B shares must be deposited into this account. The People's Bank has the authority to check these accounts on a regular basis.

According to the Shenzhen legislation, institutions permitted to act as securities firms authorised to deal in B shares are free to enter into agency agreements with foreign securities firms to handle the trading of B shares overseas. All such trading must be carried out at the Shenzhen Stock Exchange. The Shenzhen Securities Registration Company is the agency authorised to handle the registration and transfer of B shares and it records all the holders of B shares.

Shanghai Rules

The Implementing Rules of Shanghai Municipality on the Administration of Special Renminbi Share Procedures were issued by the People's Bank of China's Shanghai Branch on 25 November 1991.

The Shanghai Rules, like the Shenzhen Procedures, state that the owners of B shares enjoy the same rights as ordinary Renminbi shareholders. Like the Shenzhen Procedures, a company wishing to issue B shares must have its own independent sources of foreign exchange. The Shanghai Rules also set out certain criteria for securities institutions wishing to engage in B share trading. These institutions must:

- possess a licence to use foreign exchange in the trading of B shares;
- possess adequate telecommunications equipment and a sufficient number of employees to carry out their work; and
- enjoy authority granted by the People's Bank of China to engage in B shares business.

Records of all B share trading must be kept at least three years, and be made accessible to the relevant authorities. Of particular interest to foreign merchant bankers and financial institutions is the fact that the Shanghai Rules set forth certain criteria in respect of foreign financial institutions applying to act as brokers in the trading of B shares. They must be recommended by securities institutions in China, and sign a special agreement, and then receive approval from the authorities in charge including the People's Bank of China. Furthermore, these foreign institutions must have paid-up capital of no less than US$100 million as well as at least five years of experience in securities trading, a good business reputation and sufficient business locations as well as adequate staff.

In trading B shares, investors must open an account for the trading of B shares with the Shanghai Securities Exchange. The securities institutions approved in China may act as representatives for foreign investors opening B share accounts at the Shanghai Securities Exchange. The investor must hold a valid passport and identity card and submit these when opening his account.

As with the Shenzhen Procedures, income tax must be paid on all B share dividends and bonuses in accordance with the relevant provisions of the PRC Individual Income Tax Law and Foreign Investment Enterprise Tax Law. The payment of a stamp tax at the Shanghai Securities Exchange following each transaction is also required.

FUTURE DEVELOPMENTS

From a policy perspective, the Shanghai securities market has been receiving the greatest support from the central government in its attempt to revive Shanghai as the financial centre of China. Enterprises from throughout China may go to either Shanghai or Shenzhen in order to list on the exchange, with the eventual intention of issuing B shares in order to raise foreign funds.

The competition among foreign companies and banks to underwrite the listed B shares is becoming more and more fierce. The market situation may appear speculative at this time, and many foreign investors are particularly cautious. Nevertheless, a number of financial institutions are aggressively pursuing opportunities, as the potential of B shares is enormous. As one merchant banker in Hong Kong commented, 'We are now looking at the B share-market. We are also setting our sights for the long term, in looking and trying to find the way to get into A shares as well!'

CONCLUSION

Though foreign investors are interested in China's securities market, many still feel it is not the right time for them to participate. To address these concerns, China is making efforts to enact related legislation and improve the operation and management of listed companies and foreign exchange control, as well as the standardisation of public share issues. Experts say the most important thing is to enact and perfect securities laws and regulations to create an attractive legal climate for foreign capital to come into China's securities market. To attract investors, China is taking measures to upgrade the performance of listed companies, standardise the publication of information on them and manage the distribution of profits in a bid to raise the return on investment.

Major steps are being implemented to relax control of foreign exchange and turn the Renminbi into a convertible currency. In fact, China's economy is growing at a fast rate, and its foreign exchange reserves top US$60 billion (including private foreign exchange savings)—a great capability with which to increase foreign trade and repay external debts. The Renminbi has now virtually met the requirements of a convertible currency. Some countries and regions bordering on China have begun using Renminbi as a convertible currency with billions of Renminbi circulating outside China. The convertibility of Renminbi will remove a big road-block and allow vast amounts of foreign capital to flow into the Chinese securities markets. Foreign investors would then be able to freely repatriate their profits, dividends and interest from China, and A and B shares could be smoothly exchanged.

Some businesses in China have issued a combination of shares including State shares, legal entity shares, and public shares, but stipulated that State shares must be accounted for as shares that are not to be listed and circulated on the market. Such outdated activities are not in keeping with international practice, and have given foreign investors a bad impression. Such activities put pressure on the authorities to find solutions and establish market regulations that foreign investors can accept.

CHAPTER 17
TAXATION

Following major policy debates over the validity of adopting taxation practices of other countries, such as the United States, China's Taxation Bureau, Ministry of Finance, State Council of Legal Affairs Bureau and National People's Congress Legislative Committee worked throughout 1993 to implement a series of dramatic measures which have completely reformed China's taxation system. In December 1993, the work undertaken during the year was made public. China's government announced that, commencing 1 January 1994, the new taxation system would be applied across China. The measures attempted to bring the systems which applied separately to foreign investment enterprises and domestic enterprises in line to create a more equal system for all.

China implemented a comprehensive, full-scale and structural reform of its commercial and industrial taxation system to adapt it to the market economy and bring it in harmony with the prevailing international tax system. The new turnover tax system consisting of Value Added Tax, Consumption Tax and Business Tax came into effect on 1 January 1994, and is uniformly applicable to domestic enterprises, enterprises with foreign investment and foreign enterprises. The former Consolidated Industrial and Commercial Tax imposed on enterprises with foreign investment and foreign enterprises was rescinded and a Special Agricultural Products Tax (formerly the Product Tax) was imposed on products of agriculture, forestry, animal husbandry and water. Following the reforms, the overall tax burden remains almost the same.

VALUE ADDED TAX (VAT)

VAT is levied on production, wholesale and retail sales, importation of goods and provision of processing, and repair and replacement services. The mode of one basic rate plus one lower rate is adopted as the VAT rate. The basic rate is 17% but there is also a lower rate of 13%. The lower rate applies to basic foodstuffs and agricultural production materials, etc. Exported goods are exempt.

VAT is calculated on the basis of tax-exclusive prices which means that VAT is collected from the commodity prices excluding VAT at the stipulated rate. When goods are sold at stages prior to retail sales, a special VAT invoice is used, on which the VAT and VAT-exclusive prices have to be separately indicated. The invoices used for retail will not separately indicate the VAT for retail sales. For those taxpayers whose annual sales are less than the specified amount or who have unsophisticated accounting systems, a simpler way of collecting a fixed rate on the gross sales will be employed.

The new VAT system requires normal VAT taxpayers to make special tax registration and use special VAT invoices to enable a strict tax administration. Mechanisms are being implemented to cross-audit both sellers and buyers.

The tax burden on enterprises with foreign investment and on foreign enterprises changed after the tax reform. To ensure continuity and the consistency of the open-door policy with foreign-related tax policies, such enterprises approved before 31 December 1993 have been allowed a refund of the new VAT, Consumption Tax and Business Tax. Enterprises approved to be established after 1 January 1994 are subject to the new taxes.

CONSUMPTION TAX AND BUSINESS TAX

Consumption tax is levied on 11 consumer items: tobacco, alcohol, cosmetics, skin-care and hair-care products, precious jewellery and precious jade and stones, firecrackers and fireworks, gasoline, diesel oil, motor vehicle tyres, motorcycles and motor cars.

The amount of the tax levied is based on either the amount-on-volume method or a fixed rate based on the sales price. In the latter case, tax is calculated on the basis of the sales price including Consumption Tax but excluding VAT.

The reformed Business Tax is levied on nine items at the three tax rates; items liable include the provision of taxable services, the transfer of intangible property and sales of immovable property. The rates are 3% for transportation, communication, culture and sports; 5% for finance and insurance, the provision of taxable services, transfer of intangible property and sales of immovable property; while for entertainment the tax rates will be from 5% to 20%. All entities or individuals engaged in the above-mentioned businesses, transfer or sales activities should calculate and pay Business Tax on the basis of their respective turnovers.

INCOME TAX PAYABLE BY ENTERPRISE

From 1 January 1994, the income taxes of State-owned enterprises, collectively-owned enterprises and privately-owned enterprises (uniformly referred to as domestic enterprises) were unified to apply one flat tax rate of 33%, with deductions unified and regulated by tax laws. Periods of depreciation may be shortened and loan interests may be listed as expenses.

The Income Tax Law of the People's Republic of China for Enterprises with Foreign Investments and Foreign Enterprises promulgated in 1991 remains effective for foreign-related enterprises. The next target of income tax reform is to unify the taxes of domestic and foreign enterprises.

INCOME TAX PAYABLE BY INDIVIDUALS

The Individual Income Tax Law of the People's Republic of China passed by the Third Plenary Session of the Standing Committee of the Fifth National People's Congress and amended by the Fourth Plenary Session of the Standing Committee of the Eighth National People's Congress entered into force on 1 January 1994. Its key points are as outlined below.

(1) *Taxpayers*: individual income tax is levied in accordance with the provisions of this law on individuals who have domicile in China, or though without domicile have resided for one year or more in China on their income derived from sources within and outside China. This provision of the Individual Income Tax Law has unified the previously separate three taxes of Individual Income Regulatory Tax on Chinese residents, Individual Income Tax on foreigners and Income Tax on Industrial and Commercial Individual Households.

(2) *Level of deduction*: for income from wages and salaries, a monthly deduction of 800 yuan is allowed for expenses. But for taxpayers not domiciled in China but who derive wages and salaries from sources within China—namely, the foreigners who come to China to work—an extra 3200 yuan shall be deducted in addition to 800 yuan expenses.

(3) *Income from wages and salaries*: taxed at progressive rates ranging from 5% to 45%. Income from an author's remuneration is taxed at a flat rate of 20%; the amount of tax payable, however, is reduced by 30%. Income from remuneration for personal

services, royalties, interest, dividends, bonuses, lease of property and transfer of property, as well as contingent income and other income is taxed at a flat rate of 20%. Eight hundred yuan is deducted if the income from remuneration for personal services, author's remuneration, royalties, lease of property or transfer of property does not exceed 4000 yuan; 20% is deducted if the income exceeds 4000 yuan; the amount after the above-mentioned deductions are made is regarded as taxable income.

(4) *Remuneration for personal services*: for amounts between 20,000 and 50,000 yuan, an extra 50% is levied; 100% is levied if taxable income is in excess of 50,000 yuan.

RESOURCES TAX

The Provisional Regulations of the People's Republic of China on Resource Tax were passed by the Twelfth Standing Session of the State Council on 26 November 1993, and came into effect on 1 January 1994. Those liable to pay this tax include all entities and individuals engaged in the exploitation of mineral products or production of salt within China, including enterprises with foreign investment, foreign enterprises, administrative or military units, institutions and individuals. Taxable items include coal, crude oil, natural gas, ferrous metal ores, other non-metal ores, non-ferrous metal ores and salt.

The tax payable is calculated by the amount-on-volume method at different amounts within a prescribed range. Different tax amounts are levied for the same resource product at different stages of exploitation or production.

LAND APPRECIATION TAX

Land Appreciation Tax is only imposed on the transfer of State-owned land; collectively-owned land cannot be transferred before requisition by the State. It is only imposed on the transfer of land for payment. Transfers in other ways such as inheritance or donation without payment are exempted from the tax. Land Appreciation Tax was collected from 1 January 1994.

Taxpayers include all entities and individuals receiving proceeds from the transfer of State-owned land use rights, buildings and their attached facilities including administrative units, institutions, military units, enterprises and industrial and commercial households and other domestic units and individuals; enterprises with foreign investment, foreign enterprises and foreign organisations, overseas Chinese, residents from Hong Kong and Macau and foreign citizens.

Tax Rates

Land appreciation amount is the balance of proceeds received by the taxpayer on the transfer of real estate after deducting the sum of deductible items. A progressive tax rate is adopted for Land Appreciation Tax.

(1) For that part of the appreciation amount not exceeding 50% of the sum of deductible items, the tax rate is 30%.

(2) For that part of the appreciation amount exceeding 50%, but not exceeding 100% of the sum of deductible items, the tax rate is 40%.

(3) For that part of the appreciation amount exceeding 100%, but not exceeding 200% of the sum of deductible items, the tax rate is 50%.

(4) For that part of the appreciation amount exceeding 200% of the sum of deductible items, the tax rate is 60%.

Deductible Items

The deductible items, when computing the appreciation amount, are as follows:

- the sum paid for the acquisition of land use rights;
- costs and expenses for the development of land;
- costs and expenses for the construction of new buildings and facilities, or the assessed value for used properties and buildings;
- the tax related to the transfer of real estate; and
- other deductible items as stipulated by the Ministry of Finance.

Method of Payment

Taxpayers should notify the local competent tax authorities where the real estate is located within seven days of signing the real estate transfer agreement. Meanwhile, taxpayers should submit to the competent local tax authorities the Certificate of Property Right of the transferred real estate and building, Certificate of Land Use Right, the contract for the transfer of the land or the sale of the real estate, the report of the assessed value on real estate and other relevant materials.

Taxpayers must pay the Land Appreciation Tax determined by the tax authorities and within the period specified. Taxpayers should, after paying the taxes in accordance with the tax law, take the tax payment receipt to the relevant administration of houses and land management to go through the formalities of the change of property rights.

FURTHER TAX REFORMS

Other measures include abolishing the City Real Estate Tax and the Land Usage Fee imposed on enterprises with foreign investment, foreign enterprises or foreign individuals. New taxes include the House Property Tax, Vehicles and Vessels Tax, Land Usage Tax, City Maintenance and Construction Tax imposed on all Chinese or foreign taxpayers, as well as a levy of Security Transaction Tax and Inheritance Tax. Some of the above-mentioned taxes have been introduced and others will be gradually put into practice in the future. The old laws or regulations stay effective until the new ones are promulgated.

For foreign enterprises, the taxes that still apply include City Real Estate Tax (promulgated by the State Council on 8 August 1951), The Plate Usage Tax for Vehicles and Ships (3 April 1951), Stamp Tax (6 August 1988) and Slaughter Tax (December 1950).

PREFERENTIAL POLICIES FOR FOREIGN INVESTORS

Preferential policies towards foreign-related enterprises under the new tax system remain unchanged on the whole. After the new taxes were implemented, the tax burden of most of the foreign-related enterprises decreased or remained unchanged; only a small proportion of foreign-related enterprises experienced a tax increase. For the purpose of stabilising tax rates and protecting the economic interests of foreign-related enterprises, the State Council declared a refund of excess taxes paid before the tax reform on condition that such refunds are limited to a maximum of five years from 1994 to 1998.

Preferential policies, such as exemption from turnover tax on imported capital goods as investment including machinery, apparatus and spare parts, and on raw materials imported for producing exported products, were abrogated from 1 April 1996. Turnover taxes are exempted for all goods entering the bonded area from outside China or exported or produced from areas other than the bonded area and sold in the bonded area.

Banks with approved foreign investment in the Special Economic Zones (SEZs) or Pudong New Area are exempted from turnover taxes for five years from the beginning of their operations.

FOREIGN ENTERPRISE INCOME TAX

The Income Tax Law of the People's Republic of China for Enterprises with Foreign Investment and Foreign Enterprises and the Detailed Rules and Regulations for its implementation stipulate that:

'The State shall, in accordance with the industrial policies, guide the orientation of foreign investment and encourage the establishment of enterprises with foreign investment which adopt advanced technology and equipment and export all or greater part of their products. Such enterprises which request preferential treatments in relation to enterprise income tax shall be treated in accordance with the relevant laws and administration regulations promulgated by the State.'

Reductions and Exemptions

The exemption or reduction of local income tax on any enterprise with foreign investment which operates in an industry or undertakes a project encouraged by the State is at the discretion of the people's government of the province, autonomous region or municipality directly under the central government.

Enterprises with foreign investment established in SEZs, foreign enterprises which have establishments or places in SEZs that are engaged in production or business operations, and enterprises with foreign investment of a production nature in Economic and Technological Development Zones, are subject to levies at the reduced rate of 15%; enterprises with foreign investment of a production nature established in coastal economic open zones or in the old urban districts of cities where the SEZs or the Economic and Technological Development Zones are located are taxed at the reduced rate of 24%.

Any enterprise with foreign investment of a production nature scheduled to operate for a period of not less than 10 years will be exempted from income tax in the first and second years of profit and allowed a 15% reduction in the third to fifth profit years. However, the income tax exemption or reduction for enterprises with foreign investment engaged in the exploitation of resources such as petroleum, natural gas, and rare and precious metals is regulated separately by the State Council.

Enterprises with foreign investment which actually operate for a period of less than 10 years, repay the amount of income tax exempted or reduced.

'Enterprises of a production nature' mentioned above refer to the enterprises engaged in the following:

- machine-building and electronics industries;
- energy industries (not including oil and natural gas exploitation);
- metallurgical, chemical and building material industries;
- light, textiles and packaging industries;
- medical apparatus and pharmaceutical industries;
- agriculture, forestry, animal husbandry, fishery and water conservancy;
- construction industries;
- communications and transportation industries (not including passenger transportation);
- development of science and technology, geological survey and industrial information consultancies that are directly linked to production, and maintenance and repair services for production equipment and precision instruments; and
- other industries that are recognised by the competent department for tax affairs under the State Council.

Reductions in Special Zones

The income tax on enterprises with foreign investment in coastal economic open zones, in the old urban districts of cities where the SEZs or the Economic and Technological Development Zones are located or in other regions defined by the State Council, within the scope of energy, communications, harbour, wharf or other projects encouraged by the State, may be levied at the reduced rate of 15%. The following enterprises are eligible.

(1) Enterprises with foreign investment of a production nature established in the coastal economic areas, the SEZs, or in the old urban districts of cities where the Economic and Technological Development Zones are located, and engaged in technology-intensive or knowledge-intensive projects, projects with foreign investment of US$30 million and more, and with long pay-back periods, or energy, transportation and port construction projects.

(2) Chinese–foreign equity joint ventures engaged in port and wharf construction.

(3) Foreign banks, branches of foreign banks, banks with Chinese and foreign joint investment, and other financial institutions established in the SEZs and other areas approved by the State Council, with the capital put up by the foreign investors or operating funds appropriated by the head office amounting to US$10 million and more; and with the period of operation exceeding 10 years.

(4) Enterprises with foreign investment recognised as new, and high-technology enterprises, which are established in the New and High-Technology Industrial Development Zones approved by the State Council; and enterprises with foreign investment recognised as new-technology enterprises established in the Beijing New-technology Industrial Development Experimental Zones.

(5) Enterprises with foreign investment engaged in projects encouraged by the State and established in other areas designated by the State Council.

Enterprises with foreign investment engaged in industries that fall under item (1) will, after applying to the State Administration for Taxation for approval, pay enterprise income tax at the reduced rate of 15%.

Other Preferential Treatment

The relevant regulations, promulgated by the State Council before the entry into force of the Income Tax Law, provide preferential treatment in the form of exemption from or reduction of income tax on enterprises engaged in energy, communications, harbour, wharf and other major projects of a production nature for a period longer than that specified in the preceding section. Preferential treatment in the form of exemption from or reduction of income tax on enterprises engaged in major projects of a non-production nature will remain applicable after this law enters into force. Preferential treatments are enjoyed by the following enterprises.

(1) Chinese–foreign equity joint ventures engaged in the construction of harbours or wharves with the period of operation exceeding 15 years may, upon approval of their application by the competent tax authorities, from the year in which they begin to make a profit, be exempted from the enterprise income tax in the first five years and pay the tax at a reduced rate of 15% from the sixth to the tenth years of their operation.

(2) Foreign investment enterprises established in Hainan SEZ which engage in such infrastructural projects as airport, harbour, wharf,

railway, highway, power station, coal mine, water conservancy, etc., or in the development and operation of agriculture, and with the scheduled period of operation exceeding 15 years may, upon approval of their applications by the Hainan tax authorities, from the year in which they begin to make a profit, be exempted from the tax for the first five years and pay the enterprise income tax at the reduced rate of 15% from the sixth to the tenth years of their operations.

(3) Enterprises with foreign investment established in the Shanghai Pudong New Area and engaged in the construction of such energy and transportation projects as airport, harbour, railway, highway, and power station, etc. and with an operating period exceeding 15 years may, upon approval of their applications by the Shanghai Municipality Tax Authorities, enjoy exemption from enterprise income tax from the first profit-making year to the fifth year, and a reduction in the tax by 50% from the sixth to the tenth years.

(4) Enterprises with foreign investment exceeding US$5 million established in the SEZs and engaged in service industries, and an operating period exceeding 10 years may, upon approval of their applications by the relevant SEZ tax authorities, enjoy exemption from enterprise income tax for the first profit-making year, and a reduction in the tax by 50% for the second and third years.

(5) Foreign banks, branches of foreign banks, banks with Chinese and foreign joint investment, and other financial institutions established in the SEZs and other areas approved by the State Council, with the capital put in by foreign investors, or the operation funds appropriated by the head offices of foreign banks, exceeding US$10 million, and with an operating period lasting 10 years and more may, upon approval of their applications by the relevant tax authorities, enjoy exemption from enterprise income tax for the first profit-making year and a reduction in the tax by 50% for the second and third years.

(6) Chinese–foreign equity joint ventures recognised as new and high-technology enterprises established in the New and High-technology Industrial Development Zones approved by the State Council, with an operating period exceeding 10 years may, upon approval of their applications by the local tax authorities, enjoy exemption from enterprise income tax for the first and second profit-making years. For enterprises with foreign investment established in the SEZs and the Economic and Technological Development Zones, the preferential tax provisions for such Zones still apply. For enterprises with foreign investment established in

the Beijing New-technology Industrial Development Experimental Zone, the preferential tax provisions of the Beijing New-technology Industrial Development Experimental Zones apply.

(7) Export-oriented enterprises with foreign investment may, upon the expiration of the tax exemption and reduction period as provided for in the tax law, further enjoy a 50% reduction in enterprise income tax based on the rate stipulated by the tax law, if the value of their exports for the year exceeds 70% of the total value of products for the year. But for the SEZs and the Economic and Technological Development Zones and other export-oriented enterprises where enterprise income tax has already been reduced to 15% and the above requirements are met, the enterprise income tax is levied at 10%.

(8) Technologically advanced enterprises with foreign investment may, upon the expiration of the enterprise income tax exemption and reduction period as stipulated by the tax law, further enjoy a 50% reduction in enterprise income tax for three years based on the rate stipulated by the tax law, if they remain technologically advanced enterprises.

Other regulations relating to the exemption and reduction of enterprise income tax, having been promulgated or having been approved to promulgate by the State Council, may also apply. In applying for enterprise income tax exemption/reduction outlined in items (6), (7) and (8), enterprises with foreign investment should submit the relevant certifying documents issued by the department responsible to the local tax authorities for examination and approval.

Refund of Tax on Reinvestments

Any foreign investor in an enterprise which reinvests its share of the profit to increase the capital of the enterprise, or uses the profit as capital investment to establish other enterprises to operate for a period of not less than five years, can apply for a 10% refund of the income tax already paid on the reinvested amount.

Where other preferential provisions are provided by the State Council, such provisions shall apply. Thus a foreign investor who makes direct reinvestment in establishing or expanding an export-oriented enterprise or a technologically advanced enterprise in China, or who reinvests profit from an enterprise in Hainan SEZ directly into enterprises engaged in infrastructure and agricultural development in the same Zone, may receive a full refund of enterprise income tax paid on the reinvested amount.

Foreign investors should, within one year from the date the funds are actually injected, apply to the original tax collecting authorities for a tax refund and submit a document certifying the amount and duration of the added or new capital investment, or submit a document issued by the relevant examination and confirmation department certifying the newly established or expanded enterprise as being an export-oriented or technologically advanced enterprise.

Foreign investors must repay 60% of the refunded tax amount if the enterprises established or expanded by direct reinvestment do not meet the standards for export-oriented enterprises within three years of commencement of production or operation, or if the enterprises do not continue to be confirmed as technologically advanced enterprises. Foreign investors must repay all the refunded tax if they withdraw the reinvestment within five years.

Losses and Depreciation

Losses incurred in a tax year by any enterprise with foreign investment, or by an establishment or a place set up in China by a foreign enterprise to engage in production or business operations, may be made up by the income of the following tax year. Should the income of the following tax year be insufficient to make up for the said losses, the balance may be made up by its income in the next subsequent year, and so on, over a period not exceeding five years.

Foreign investment enterprises may, after applying to the local tax authorities for examination and upon approval by the State Administration of Taxation, shorten the period of depreciation for:

(1) machinery and equipment that are subject to strong corrosion by acid or alkali, and factory buildings and structures that are constantly subjected to vibration;

(2) machinery and equipment that are constantly running round the clock for the purpose of raising the utilisation rate or increasing the intensity of usage; and

(3) fixed assets of a Chinese–foreign contractual joint venture with the period of cooperation shorter than the depreciation periods as specified in the regulations, which will be left with the Chinese party upon the termination of the venture.

Consolidated Returns

Any enterprise with foreign investment is allowed, when filing a consolidated income tax return, to deduct from the amount of tax payable the foreign income tax already paid abroad in respect of the income derived from sources outside China. The deductible amount must, however, not exceed the amount of income tax payable under the tax law in respect of the income derived from sources outside China.

Any foreign enterprise which has no establishment or place in China but derives profit, interests, rental, royalty and other income from sources in China, or, though it has an establishment or place in China, the said income is not effectively connected with such establishment or place, must pay an income tax of 20% on such income.

Further Exemptible Income

Income tax is reduced or exempted on the following income.

(1) The profit derived by a foreign investor from an enterprise with foreign investment is exempt from income tax.

(2) Income from interests on loans made to the Chinese government or Chinese state banks by international financial organisations is exempt from income tax.

(3) Income from interest on loans made at a preferential interest rate to Chinese state banks by foreign banks is exempt from income tax.

(4) Income tax on the royalties received for the supply of technical know-how on scientific research, exploitation of energy resources, development of the communications industries, agricultural, forestry and animal husbandry production, and the development of important technologies may, upon approval by the competent department for tax affairs under the State Council, be levied at the reduced rate of 10%. Where the technology supplied is advanced or the terms are preferential, exemption from income tax may be allowed.

INCOME TAX ON ROYALTIES

Reduction or exemption of income tax on royalties as provided above applies to the following areas.

(1) Royalties obtained from the provision of the following proprietary technology to the farming, forestry, animal husbandry and fishery industries: technology to improve soil and grassland, to reclaim and develop barren hills, and to fully restore them to their natural condition; to nurture new species and varieties of fauna and flora

and to produce high-efficiency but low-toxicity agricultural chemicals; to provide the farming, forestry, animal husbandry and fishery industries with scientific production and management techniques; to preserve the ecological balance; and to increase China's capability of fighting natural disasters.

(2) Royalties obtained from the provision of proprietary technology to academies of science, colleges and universities, and other institutions of higher learning and scientific research to conduct, or to cooperate in the conduct of, scientific research or scientific experiments.

(3) Royalties obtained from the provision of proprietary technology for the exploitation of energy resources and the development of communications and transportation.

(4) Royalties obtained from the provision of proprietary technology in energy conservation and the prevention and control of environmental pollution.

(5) Royalties obtained from the provision of proprietary technology in the development of the following important fields of technology:

- important advanced technology in the production of mechanical and electronic equipment;
- nuclear power technology;
- technology in the production of large-scale integrated circuits;
- technology in the production of photo-integration microwave semiconductors and microwave integrated circuits and microwave tubes;
- technology in the manufacturing of high-speed electronic computers and microprocessors;
- optical telecommunications technology;
- remote ultra-high voltage direct current electricity transmission technology; and
- technology in the liquefaction, gasification and integrated utilisation of coal.

The profit (dividends) derived from other investment enterprises may be excluded from the taxable income of the foreign investment enterprise, but the cost and loss incurred in the above-mentioned investments may not be deducted from the taxable income. After adjustment, tariff rates are decreased as a whole, which lowers the costs when foreign investment enterprises import raw materials and spare parts. The stipulation that foreign investment enterprises can no longer import tariff-free motor cars will not seriously affect them after the tariff rate for motor cars decreases.

TAX TREATMENT OF INTANGIBLE ASSETS AND ESTABLISHMENT COSTS

Amortisation of intangible assets such as patents, proprietary technology, trademarks, copyright, and right to the use of sites are computed by the straight-line method. Intangible assets, put in as investment or acquired with the right to use, may be amortised according to the stipulated time-limit, if a time-limit for the usage is provided for in the agreement or contract. Intangible assets without such a stipulated time-limit, or being self-developed, are amortised over a period of not less than 10 years.

Reasonable exploration expenses incurred by an enterprise engaged in exploitation of petroleum resources may be amortised from the revenues generated from the oil (or gas) field that has gone into commercial production, but the amortisation period shall not be less than one year. If a contract area owned by a foreign oil company terminates its operation due to its failure to find any oil (or gas) of commercial value, and if it does not continue to own any contract area for exploitation of oil (or gas) resources or maintain any operation in China, reasonable exploration expenses incurred in the terminated contract area may be amortised. Examination and confirmation of the expenses and the issue of a certifying document by the relevant tax authorities is required. Such amortisation must be from the production income generated from any newly owned contract area, where a new oil (or gas) cooperative exploitation contract is signed within 10 years of the termination of the old contract.

Expenses incurred while preparing to establish an enterprise may be amortised starting from the month following that in which it goes into production or business; however, the amortisation period cannot be less than five years.

DOUBLE TAXATION AGREEMENTS

The Sino-Japan Taxation Agreement concluded on 6 September 1983 and entering into force on 1 January 1985 was the first comprehensive agreement for the avoidance of double taxation signed between China and another country. The following principles are embodied in this agreement.

The profits of an enterprise of a contracting state are taxable only in that contracting state unless the enterprise carries on business in the other contracting state through a permanent establishment situated there. The reduction and exemption on the profits of an enterprise of a contracting state are regarded by the other contracting state as a tax deduction, thereby observing the principle of tax sparing credit, with scope limited to the reduction, exemption and tax refund for reinvestment provisions of the Chinese tax laws and detailed rules and regulations for implementation.

A fixed tax rate deduction is provided in the agreement for the income from investment, that is, if a resident of a contracting state receives income from investment from the other contracting state, and no matter whether the other contracting state grants a reduction or exemption to the resident in accordance with its domestic tax law or imposes tax at the prescribed tax rate in accordance with the agreement, the other contracting state will, in calculating the income tax payable, deduct the amount at the tax rate prescribed in the agreement. It is provided in the Sino-Japan tax agreement that the following deduction rates be adopted: 10% for dividends paid by joint ventures, 20% for other dividends, 10% for interest and 20% for royalties.

FOREIGN INVESTORS AND CHINA'S TAXATION SYSTEM

Foreign investors went into momentary shock following China's December 1993 announcement, unsure of the ramifications of such a radical overhaul of the system. In the past, China had adopted a cautious, step-by-step approach to passing legislation by first adopting a law and setting out general principles. More detailed regulations followed, filling in the gaps. China's 1993 taxation reforms adopted a new approach. The entire legislative system for reforming and implementing the new taxation system was introduced at one time. While foreign investors may have reeled initially, the speed with which the reforms came into place provided at once a clear and concise system, without speculation on future legislation, thereby achieving the goal of providing clarity and, in turn, confidence in the new system.

In 1994, China's taxation authorities declared that China's full-scale taxation reform would not place a significant burden on foreign investment enterprises. Foreign investment enterprises would continue to enjoy the same kinds of preferential treatment on tax as in the past. Taxation reform would ensure that China's policy of opening to the outside world would continue through the provision of preferential treatment for foreign investors—specifically, the former income tax reductions enjoyed by foreign investment enterprises in the SEZs, Economic and Technological Development Zones and open coastal areas remain valid. Income tax applied to foreign investment enterprises under the new overall taxation regime continues to be handled separately as stipulated in the Foreign Investment and Foreign Enterprises Tax Law promulgated on 9 April 1991. This legislation was initially drafted to attract foreign investment in the wake of events in China in 1989.

In fact, the tax position of foreign investment enterprises today remains the same as before the reforms, namely, 33% in most areas of China with a preferential rate of only 15% in many of the special zones and coastal areas mentioned above. Prior to the 1993 reforms, domestic Chinese enterprises were burdened with a tax rate of 55%, which was an incentive for many to enter into fake joint ventures with their own offshore subsidiaries for the purpose of avoiding tax. Domestic enterprises are now taxed at the same rate as foreign investment enterprises.

Investor Concerns

Despite the enormous strides made under the recent reforms, foreign investors have, however, been concerned and often confused by the handling of certain matters. The income tax and reductions on foreign investment enterprises remain the same but the turnover tax on foreign investment enterprises has been changed. The previous Industrial and Commercial Consolidated Tax has been replaced by the Turnover Tax. In China, VAT and Business Tax are now together called Turnover Tax. The Regulations on how Foreign Investment Enterprises are to apply the new Turnover Tax, promulgated by the National People's Congress on 29 December 1993, caused some foreign investment enterprises concern as to whether they would pay a higher turnover tax.

Taking these concerns into consideration, the Chinese tax authorities have given foreign investment enterprises established before 31 December 1993, a special benefit. They are eligible to have any additional tax burden resulting from the new legislation refunded in a lump sum at the end of the year, or in instalments over the year in which approval for such a refund by the department in charge has been obtained. Depending on the operations concerned, such refunds may be given for terms up to as much as five years.

This consideration allows a transfer period for those enterprises which had calculated their feasibility of operations prior to the introduction of the new taxation system. Foreign investment enterprises, however, that were not approved prior to 1 January 1994 may not obtain such a refund and are required to pay turnover taxes in accordance with the new legislation.

Export Tax

Before 1994, export products of foreign investment enterprises were exempt from Consolidated Industrial and Commercial Tax. In the regulations for the implementation of the law on Chinese–foreign equity joint ventures, Article 72 states that, 'Except those export items restricted by the State, products of Joint Venture for export shall be exempt from the Consolidated Industrial and Commercial Tax', while products sold on the domestic market were subject to this tax. On 1 January 1994, the new Value Added Tax (VAT) was introduced to replace the Consolidated Industrial and Commercial Tax.

Most foreign investment enterprises hoped that the previous exemption from the Consolidated Industrial and Commercial Tax provided in respect of exports would continue in the form of a refund of taxes, paid in respect of exports under the new VAT. However, on 25 August 1994, the Notice on Export Tax Refund of Foreign Investment Enterprises (the Notice) was promulgated by the Ministry of Finance and the State Taxation Bureau. In accordance with the Notice, VAT and Consumption Tax on export products of foreign investment enterprises are exempted, but the taxable amount for purchase of raw materials is not refundable. This provides some disadvantage compared to domestic enterprises where the taxable amount on the purchase of raw materials can be refunded.

In respect of the difference between VAT and Consolidated Industrial and Commercial Tax, the tax burden on foreign investment enterprises has been changed, as the concept of both taxes is essentially different. In the past, the average Consolidated Industrial and Commercial Tax was about 14%, whereas VAT is about 17%.

Initially, the Notice was issued without clarification as to how it should be applied by foreign investment enterprises. The Notice seemed to suggest that all foreign investment enterprises would be required to comply with it; in the following few months, however, it was observed that only enterprises established before 31 December 1993 were actually bound by the Notice. Foreign investment enterprises established after 1 January 1994 are allowed to enjoy the same treatment as domestic enterprises. They have the right to a refund on the taxable amount for purchases of raw materials from the domestic market as part of the production chain for export.

VAT Round-up

As for foreign investment enterprises established before 31 December 1993, the tax on products of foreign investment enterprises for export differed from that of domestic enterprises. Foreign investment enterprises have become less competitive in respect of exports, and whereas domestic enterprises enjoyed a tax rebate on raw materials used in the production of export products, foreign investment enterprises did not.

In the interest of fairness in a competitive market, and given the adoption of equitable economic policies in China, the Chinese authorities have cancelled the tax required to be paid by foreign investment enterprises on raw materials to be used in the production of export products. The end result of this, in effect, is a nationwide system of even tax treatment for foreign investment enterprises and domestic enterprises in respect of VAT, even if it is expressed in different terms for each.

CONCLUSION

To encourage foreign investments and to be able to rely on taxation as the main budgetary tool, the Chinese government has been making efforts since 1983 to carry out reforms. This has in turn required an overhaul of the commercial and individual taxation systems.

In addition, a number of preferential tax policies have been adjusted to put foreign investment and domestic enterprises on the same level. Under the existing tax system, foreign enterprises may obtain reductions and exemptions on turnover tax and income tax in accordance with the relevant laws and regulations promulgated by the State Council. At present, foreign and domestic enterprises in China are receiving the same tax treatment in all respects.

PART 5

INTELLECTUAL PROPERTY AND TECHNOLOGY TRANSFER

CHAPTER 18

TRADEMARKS

In 1978, China opened up to the outside world, and its laws regulating foreign investment had to be revised. Consequently, two pieces of legislation were drafted by the State Administration for Industry and Commerce (the SAIC) to revise the 1963 Trademark Law. *The Trademark Law of the People's Republic of China* (the Trademark Law) was implemented in March 1983. It was later repealed and updated by new implementing regulations, which were approved by the State Council on 3 January 1988, and promulgated by the SAIC on 18 January 1988. Amendments to the Trademark Law were subsequently made, according to the Decision on the Revision of the Trademark Law of the People's Republic of China in February 1993. The amended law came into effect on 1 July 1993.

The 1993 Trademark Law was a modern piece of legislation. Before its enactment, China sent specialists overseas to research the trademark laws of Japan, the United States, and a number of European countries. In addition, it sought advice from the World Intellectual Property Organisation (WIPO) of the United Nations. The Trademark Law resulted in five major developments:

- the emergence of the concept of exclusive right;
- the replacement of a compulsory registration system with a voluntary system;
- new procedures for trademark application, examination and registration;
- the linking of trademark rights to quality control; and
- China's membership of the Paris Convention for the Protection of Industrial Property.

The concept of exclusive use is clearly recognised under the new law. Article 3 states that: 'The trademark registrant shall enjoy an exclusive right to use the trademark, which right shall be protected by the law'. Any trademark user may apply for trademark registration and, once his application is approved, he obtains the exclusive right to that mark. This right will be protected against infringement under State law.

Although the Trademark Law adopted the principle of exclusive use, it also emphasised the importance of quality control and consumer protection. It provides that the assignee of a trademark must maintain the quality of the product for which the trademark is registered. Likewise, when the trademark is licensed, the licensee must maintain the quality of the original product. However, poor quality control has been a chronic problem for Chinese enterprises. Consequently, the Trademark Law has at best played only a marginal role in controlling what is a widespread problem.

REGISTRATION

Only registered trademarks can be legally protected in China. Under the Trademark Law, a registered trademark means a 'trademark which has been approved and registered by the Trademark Office'. Consequently, registered trademarks must be marked with either the Chinese words for Registered Trademark (注册商標), or the symbol R, or TM (注). The Trademark Law does not specify any penalty for failing to comply with this requirement; however, government officials have expressed their intention to impose penalties in the near future.

Under the 1963 Trademark Regulations, which were based on the principle of quality control, trademark registration was made compulsory. When applying for registration, a form had to be submitted with the application specifying the quality of the related goods. Because of its compulsory nature, trademark registration became a burden for proprietors.

Under the Trademark Law, trademark registration is voluntary. This is due largely to the new emphasis placed on the concept of exclusive right, which differs from the 1963 Regulations' emphasis on quality control. Nevertheless, Article 5 of the Trademark Law states that certain goods may not be sold in the market unless they use registered trademarks. If goods are sold in violation of Article 5, the SAIC is empowered through its local departments to prohibit the goods from being sold. More specifically, according to Article 7 of the Implementing Regulations, pharmaceuticals and tobacco products cannot be sold unless they bear a registered trademark. In the case of pharmaceuticals, Article 11 requires that a 'pharmaceutical business licence' issued by the administrative department for health be appended to the application to ensure consumer protection. In the case of tobacco products, Article 11 requires that production approval certificates issued by the State Administration for Tobacco be appended to the application.

In addition to the Implementing Regulations, the Tobacco Monopoly Regulations of the People's Republic of China require that cigarettes and cigars have registered trademarks before they are sold on the domestic market. This requirement is directed towards consumer protection and is based on the same principle of quality control imposed by the Trademark Law on pharmaceutical sales. Article 7 of the new Implementing Regulations extends to the SAIC the power to require other commodities to have registered trademarks.

Under the 1963 Regulations, once a Chinese trademark had been registered, it remained valid indefinitely. Foreign trademarks, on the other hand, had only a 10-year period of validity, which had to be renewed upon expiry. A renewal application involved the same procedure as the original application. The new Trademark Law removed this distinction by extending equal protection to both Chinese and foreign trademarks. This is implemented through the Paris Convention's principle of 'national treatment'. Under the new law, both Chinese and foreign trademarks will receive a 10-year period of validity, renewable upon expiry.

Registration can be revoked if a company does not use the registered trademark for three years or more. However, this is not as strict as it may seem: 'use' is defined rather broadly to include use in publicity, advertising, or display, including samples distributed in catalogues and product literature. Therefore, if a trademark has been used in advertisements or exhibitions within a three-year period, such use may substitute for the actual use of the trademark.

The new Trademark Law attaches great importance to safeguarding the proprietor's rights to a trademark. After registration, a trademark is protected by Chinese law: no-one can apply to register a trademark which is identical or similar to trademarks for the same or similar goods. This is emphasised in Article 17 of the Trademark Law, which states, 'Where a trademark for the registration of which has been applied for is...identical with or similar to the trademark of another person which, in respect of the same or similar goods, has been registered or, after examination, preliminarily approved, the Trademark Office shall refuse the application and shall not publish the trademark'.

THE FIRST-TO-FILE PRINCIPLE

In China, trademark rights can only be protected by registration. In this regard, it has adopted the first-to-file rule. This means that the first applicant to file and register a trademark is the one who receives rights and protections in that mark: the applicant does not have to prove ownership or prior use. In other jurisdictions, such as Hong Kong, enforceable rights may be acquired in a mark by developing a reputation in the mark through use. Such marks are called 'common law' marks. In China, however, an applicant does not have to prove ownership or prior use. Consequently, anyone can register a trademark, even if that mark is registered by a different company somewhere else in the world. As far as China is concerned, whether a trademark has already been in use is simply not a consideration.

Under Chinese law, only the holder of a trademark who has received registration approval can be the legitimate proprietor of that mark, and only the legitimate proprietor can be protected. When an application for trademark registration is approved, it automatically becomes impossible for another applicant to gain approval for the same or a similar mark on the same or similar goods. Therefore, if a trademark proprietor does not bother to apply for registration in China, someone else, even if he is not the legitimate owner, can apply and receive legal protection for that mark.

Registration in China of one form of a mark does not provide protection to any other forms of that mark. Therefore, in addition to registering the Chinese-character version, it is equally important to register the Roman-letter form of the mark. Registration in block capital letters will protect all other Roman scripts. In order to obtain the best coverage, separate registrations for the trademark should be obtained in its original Roman-letter form, in Pinyin (the official transcription of Chinese into the Roman alphabet), and in both traditional and simplified Chinese characters.

THE PARIS CONVENTION

Under the 1963 law, holders of foreign trademarks applying for registration in China had to meet two requirements:

- the applicant had to be from a country which had concluded a reciprocal trademark agreement; and
- a copy of the registration certificate from the country of origin had to be submitted.

Foreign applicants may file applications in accordance with the principle of reciprocity. This may be done according to an international treaty to which China and the country of the registrant are both parties. Therefore, any person or any legal entity may register a trademark if they belong to a country which:

- has signed a trademark agreement with China;
- has signed a reciprocal arrangement with China; or
- has joined the Paris Convention.

On 19 March 1985, China became a signatory to the Paris Convention. The purpose of the Convention is to form a union of member nations for the protection of industrial property. A country which is a signatory to the Paris Convention undertakes to grant the same rights and protections against infringement to nationals of other contracting states as it does to its own nationals.

The Paris Convention provides a means by which an applicant can apply for trademark registration in one convention country and claim that date as the priority date when filing an application in another member country. If an application has already been filed for trademark registration in a convention country, that date will be deemed to be the priority date when applying in China. The second application must be made within six months of the first. However, in China's case, Paris Convention priority claims can only be made for applications filed after 19 March 1985.

Under the Convention, nationals of all contracting states are entitled to the same legal remedies for trademark infringement. However, they must comply with the same conditions and formalities normally imposed upon nationals of the country where the infringement occurred.

TRADEMARK INFRINGEMENT

It has been reported that there have been over 10,000 trademark disputes in China. Many of these cases involved Hong Kong firms whose products are processed in China to avoid rising production costs in Hong Kong and Macau. Many factories in China have taken advantage of this trend and have begun to misappropriate trademarks in order to increase their own sales. According to Article 38 of the Trademark Law, the following acts constitute trademark infringement:

- using an identical or similar trademark on identical or similar goods;
- selling goods bearing a counterfeited registered trademark;
- making or selling representations of a registered trademark without authorisation; or

- causing prejudice to another person's exclusive right to use a registered trademark.

The scope of Article 38(4) has been extended by Article 41 of the new Implementing Regulations to include acts of distribution, packaging, storage, transportation, mailing, and concealment of infringing goods.

A party whose right has been infringed may institute proceedings directly through the People's Courts. The trial will be conducted at the intermediate court level where the infringement occurred. Any party dissatisfied with the decision may appeal to the municipal or provincial People's Courts.

Most injured parties prefer to seek administrative remedies in accordance with Article 39 of the Trademark Law. Infringement cases involving foreigners may be entrusted to the Trademark Agency of the China Council for the Promotion of International Trade (the CCPIT) in Beijing, the China Patent Agent (HK) Ltd., or other authorised agencies or firms dealing with international intellectual property business, which in turn submits them to the SAIC. An injured party may also go directly to the SAIC at or above the county level where the infringer has his domicile or establishment. Under Articles 42 and 45 of the new Implementing Regulations, 'anyone' may register a complaint with the SAIC against a trademark infringer or counterfeiter.

The SAIC has the power to halt the infringement immediately and to award compensation to the damaged party. Compensation includes either the profits that the infringers earned through infringing the trademark, or the damages suffered by the injured party. In serious circumstances, the SAIC may also impose a fine. Any party passing off the registered trademark of another party will be fined. In addition, he will have to compensate the injured party for damages suffered. 'Passing off' includes sales. Anyone directly responsible for passing off a trademark will face criminal prosecution.

The SAIC has proved effective in dealing with trademark infringements through administrative means. In order to obtain an administrative remedy, however, it is essential that the injured party's trademark be registered in China. For example, in 1982, Monsanto Co. of the United States registered 'Lasso' and its Chinese equivalent 'la suo' for herbicides. Meanwhile, another foreign company had been exporting herbicides to China since 1980 under the trademark 'Oxtaxol' or 'ao te la suo' in Chinese, but had not registered it. The Chinese version of 'Oxtaxol' incorporated the characters for 'la suo', which comprised the Chinese version of Lasso. Lasso therefore claimed that its trademark was being infringed.

In 1984, Monsanto Co. submitted its case. The SAIC immediately sent a warning letter to the infringer. The infringer refused to stop, claiming that its trademark had been in use since 1980. The SAIC responded by explaining that prior registration is a principle stated in China's Trademark Law. Because Oxtaxol was not registered in China, its proprietor was compelled to alter the mark so that its characters would be substantially different from the 'la suo' used for Lasso.

The State Administration for Industry and Commerce has used persuasive means to remedy acts of trademark infringement. For example, a Japanese company which produced electrical appliances had registered its trademark in China as early as December 1976. When it learned that a Chinese enterprise was counterfeiting its goods and printing false packing cases, the Japanese company enlisted the help of the China Patent Agent, which submitted the case to the relevant SAIC office at the district level. The authorities then confiscated the counterfeit goods, and either burned the packing cases and catalogues or took them to a paper mill to be ground into pulp. The infringers later submitted letters of guarantee that they would cease their activities.

THE TRADEMARK BUREAU

The Trademark Bureau, an agency under the SAIC, is responsible for trademark registration and control in China. Any matter involving the use of, or application for, a trademark is within its jurisdiction. The actual enforcement of China's Trademark Law, however, rests with the local departments of the SAIC.

All trademark applications must be submitted to the Trademark Bureau's official agents: the Trademark Registration Agency of the CCPIT in Beijing, the China Patent Agent (HK) Ltd. (CPA) in Hong Kong, or other authorised trademark agencies dealing with international trademark matters. Under Article 3 of the Implementing Regulations, the SAIC may allow other organisations to handle foreign trademark matters on an agency basis. Although foreign applicants must appoint one of these organisations as their agent for 'handling other trademark matters', nowhere is it specified what 'handling other trademark matters' includes. In a number of cases, the CCPIT has helped foreign companies to resolve their trademark disputes in China. For example, when a Chinese factory tried to use a bottle identical to that used by Coca-Cola, the CCPIT persuaded the factory to discontinue its use. The CCPIT's argument was that the factory could certainly come up with a better design of its own.

The Trademark Bureau will not accept applications from nationals or companies from countries that do not have diplomatic relations with China. However, there is one loophole: because a company by definition is a legal entity, it may apply for a trademark without disclosing the nationality of its individual shareholders.

Making a Search

As there is no systematic recording of accepted and registered trademarks in China, there is always a degree of uncertainty as to whether or not a proposed trademark conflicts with an existing one. In most of the world's trademark systems, there is a facility whereby searches can be conducted to see if the same, or a similar, trademark has already been registered. At present, there is no possible way to conduct pre-application searches in China. However, there are two places where one can search for an existing trademark: the *Quan Guo Zhu Ce Shang Biao Ming Cheng Hui Bian* (Directory of Registered Trademarks), and the *Shangbiao Gonggao* (Trademark Gazette). The Directory lists trademarks registered during the 50 years preceding July 1981. However, it contains only written descriptions of the marks and the classes under which they fall; there is no visual representation.

According to Article 43 of the Trademark Law, all trademarks registered under the 1963 Regulations are still valid, and these should all be registered in the Trademark Gazette. Unfortunately, the Gazette, like so many other publications, was suspended during the Cultural Revolution, so trademarks registered during that period are not recorded. The Gazette publishes trademarks which have been accepted. If no opposition is filed within three months, the trademark owner receives a certificate of registration valid for 10 years. The Gazette is published every two weeks, but only in Chinese. An applicant who cannot read Chinese must therefore request an official agent to do a search. While this may be done directly through the Trademark Bureau in Beijing, such enquiries are not encouraged. Due to these problems, and because the examination process to date has not been particularly stringent, most foreign applicants skip the search and go directly to registration.

Filing an Application

Trademark applications may be filed by the Trademark Bureau's official agents, the CCPIT in Beijing, the CPA in Hong Kong, or any organisation designated by the SAIC. A separate signed application must be submitted for each trademark, and for each individual class of goods covered by the trademark. Unlike international practice, if the applicant wishes to use a registered trademark on another product, he must file a separate application, even if it is in the same class as the original. Every application must comprise the application form, a power of attorney and specimen marks.

According to Article 14 of the Implementing Regulations, all three documents, if in a foreign language, must be accompanied by a Chinese translation. Applicants who do not read or write Chinese must either find legal counsel who can act on their behalf, or use the translation service provided by the Trademark Bureau's agents for an extra fee.

If the owner needs to change the words or design of a registered trademark, he must submit a new registration application; if he changes his name or address, he must file an application for amendment. According to Article 20 of the Implementing Regulations, when the registrant applies for a name change, he must submit an Application Form for Changing the Name of the Trademark Registrant, and a Certificate of the Changes to the Trademark Bureau. The original Trademark Registration Licence must also be returned to the Bureau which will give the licence back to the registrant after appending and publishing the changes.

Foreign Applicants

Foreign applicants cannot deal directly with the Trademark Bureau and must appoint an agent to process the application on their behalf. This agent is invariably the China Trademark Agency (the CTMA) of the CCPIT, the CPA or the other authorised agents as described above.

The power of attorney is a form signed by the applicant authorising the agent to process the application. It must be submitted in duplicate and must also stipulate the agent's limits of authority and the consignor's nationality. According to the Implementing Regulations, the power of attorney must be notarised. Powers of attorney may also require authentication procedures, depending on whether or not there is a reciprocal arrangement between the applicant's country and China.

Trademark Specimens

Along with the trademark application, specimens of the mark must also be filed. Although Article 9 of the Implementing Regulations calls for only 10 copies of the trademark design, the CCPIT in Beijing requires 15 copies while the CPA in Hong Kong requires 15 to 20 copies, along with the standard power of attorney which authorises the CPA to act as the registration agent. The specimens must be accompanied by an explanation of the meaning of the mark and how it was derived. If the mark has no particular meaning, then nothing needs to be said. There is also no specimen requirement if the mark is represented only in block capital form. Specimens must be submitted on glossy, durable paper, not exceeding 10×10 cm. Photocopies of the trademark may be used; however, if the trademark is in colour, the specimens must also be in colour, and an additional black and white ink draft of the mark must also be submitted.

The 1988 Implementing Regulations go into even greater detail regarding specimens. Chapter II, Article 9, specifies that trademark specimens must be clear and easy to paste up, and that the length and width should not exceed 10×10 cm or be less than 5×5 cm. According to Article 10, the name of the goods must be entered in accordance with the Classification of Goods. If the item is not listed in the Classification, a description of it must be attached. In addition, the name and seal of the applicant must be consistent with the name already approved or registered in China.

Although not specified in the Implementing Regulations, a copy of the foreign applicant's business registration certificate, or certificate of incorporation, may be required by the Trademark Bureau if the trademark is to be used on products for human use (e.g. hair products, chemicals, medicines, traditional Chinese medicines, or medicinal liquors). In such cases, the trademark application must be accompanied by a certified copy of a document proving that production of the goods has been approved in the applicant's country.

PRODUCT CLASSIFICATION

Together with the trademark application, a form must be filed stating the name of the product and the category or class in which it falls. The classes are stipulated by law. While most countries adopt the international classification system, which consists of 34 classes, China has its own classification system consisting of 78 classes—more than twice the international standard.

In the past, foreign companies circumvented this problem by registering trademarks for products which they had not produced, but anticipated that they might one day make. However, this practice was curtailed by Article 10 of the new Implementing Regulations, which states that products covered by the trademark must be within the scope of business already examined, approved or registered. Nevertheless, a trademark proprietor should still be able to file separate applications to cover as wide a range as possible of related classes of product to prevent others from registering identical marks. This is precisely what Walt Disney Co. did by having over 350 marks registered in over 50 classes.

One-Class Limitation

Under Chinese law, a single trademark registration can cover products in one class only. Therefore, a separate registration application must be filed for each class of product under which the trademark will be used. For instance, bicycles are placed in Class 19, while their fittings are scattered among Classes 19, 20 and 30. This is further complicated by the fact that a single registration is confined to one particular product and will not cover all products in any single class.

It can be a confusing process to find the proper classification for a product when registering a trademark. Each of the 78 classes has several different headings, under which there are usually lengthy lists of products. In some cases, from a Western perspective, they may bear little or no relation to the wording in the heading.

While all the headings listed under the 78 classes have been translated into English, many of the itemised products under them have not. Consequently, if a person registering a trademark cannot read Chinese, he may very easily be misled into registering an item in a class which, from the translated heading, appears to be the correct one, whereas in fact the particular item may not exist in the untranslated Chinese text below and may be listed under another heading. A case in point was a lawyer who, unfamiliar with Chinese, registered the item 'dynamometer' under Class 13, because the translated English heading read 'measuring and weighing apparatus'. Dynamometers are specifically listed in Chinese under Class 14, although the heading of Class 14 ('Wire and wireless telegraphic equipments; wireless sets; phonographs; photographical, cinematographical, optical, thermal, testing and surveying apparatus, instruments and supplies') gives no indication of this.

Chinese Method of Classification

In order to understand the Chinese method, one must realise that the classes themselves represent units of reckoning for the scope covered by each trademark applied to the goods. The Chinese use four principles in developing these classifications: raw materials, production, sale and use. Under raw materials, the similarity of goods is evaluated based on their material composition. Under the principle of sale, similarity is judged based on the sales outlet through which the goods are distributed; use determines similarity based on how the end-user uses the goods.

China's inordinate number of classifications can be largely attributed to its economic development. China's economy has traditionally been agriculture-based and underdeveloped; it made sense to classify goods based on the principles of raw materials and production. With the opening up of China and the introduction of specialised technology and an industrial economy, a host of new commodities entered the market and new trading conditions emerged. With changing consumer habits, the principles of sale and use entered the picture.

China's development in recent years has created many new forms of economy which have broken down the previous emphasis on commodity circulation, which was largely a function of the State-owned enterprises. Consequently, the original classification system, based on the principles of raw materials and production, has more or less become defunct. By continuing to divide classes of goods on the basis of production and raw materials, similar or identical goods which have the same use and sales distribution outlets will find themselves placed in different classes only because their raw materials are different. Cooking utensils are a good example of this problem—they are divided into classes based on the raw materials principle: copper hotpots are placed in Class 21, while aluminium hotpots are in Class 67; stainless steel cooking utensils are placed in Class 21, while aluminium kettles, ladles and woks are in Class 67, and iron woks and kettles are in Class 18.

According to Chinese sources which recognise the need to reform the system, it would be in China's best interests to adopt the international classification system. If China were to develop its own system from scratch, it would require about seven or eight years to complete. However, there are too many trademarks being registered in China each year to wait that long. A transfer to the international classification system could be effected within a year, but there are many practical problems involved. The placement of many products in the international classification system does not correspond with Chinese production and consumption habits. For instance, the international system divides liquor into three classes: brandy is grouped in Class 31, together with grain, livestock, fruit, vegetables, and flowers; beer is placed in Class 32, together with soft drinks; wine and liqueurs belong to Class 33. In Chinese, all alcoholic drinks are called wine (*jiu*), and are therefore placed in one class. For reasons such as this, it will be difficult for the international system to be adopted in its entirety in China without adjusting it according to the consumption habits of Chinese society.

OPPOSITION TO A TRADEMARK APPLICATION

Once a trademark application has been preliminarily approved, any person may file an objection to the trademark. According to Article 18 of the Implementing Regulations, this must be in the form of a letter of objection sent in duplicate to the Trademark Bureau. The applicant whose application is being opposed must reply to the letter within a prescribed period, or the case will go directly to the Trademark Bureau for adjudication. Whether or not an objection is successful depends on factors such as whether the trademarks are identical or similar, whether they cause confusion, or how well recognised the opposing mark is.

Objections must be lodged within three months of the date of publication. Failure to do so will leave the opposing party without a remedy. For instance, Walt Disney Co. missed the objection deadline after a Chinese manufacturer registered the words 'Mickey Mouse' along with the corresponding mouse design. Disney's only remedy was to negotiate directly and pay the Chinese manufacturer for the assignment of the trademark registration. After the assignment, Disney, in one move, filed 350 applications for the registration of its trademarks in China.

After registration, a trademark may be disputed by the prior registrant of an identical or similar trademark. However, unless the person disputing the registered mark is the registrant of an earlier registered trademark, he has no right to enter into a dispute. In order to enter into a dispute, the person making the claim must apply to the Trademark Review and Adjudication Board. This must be done within one year of the date that registration was approved.

REAPPLICATION AFTER REJECTION

If an application for trademark registration is rejected, the Trademark Review and Adjudication Board must notify the applicant in writing. Under Article 22 of the Trademark Law, a dissatisfied applicant may apply for review within 15 days of receiving the notification of rejection. However, under Article 46 of the Implementing Regulations, the applicant may, with special cause, request two extensions of the 15-day time-limit. As each extension is limited to 30 days, a dissatisfied applicant may, in reality, have 75 days within which to reapply.

According to Article 23 of the Implementing Regulations, the applicant must submit the following documents to the Trademark Review and Adjudication Board: an application form for review of a rejected application for assignment, or a rejected application for renewal of registration, as well as the original application form and rejection notification. In any application for review of a trademark, the decision of the Board is final. The chairman of the board is also the Deputy Director of Trademark Affairs at the SAIC, the body supervising the Trademark Bureau. Therefore, decisions by the Board are not subordinate to decisions by the Trademark Bureau.

LICENSING TRADEMARKS

Any trademark registered in China may be licensed. The trademark registrant may authorise other persons to use his registered trademark simply by signing a trademark licensing contract. Duplicate copies of the contract must be submitted to both the Trademark Bureau and the SAIC; no special forms or separate licensing contracts are required. Licences are frequently included in joint venture of technology transfer contracts.

If the contract has not been approved by a high-level State agency, it should be notarised in China. Notarisation will help prevent possible future disputes as it is evidence of the licence's legitimacy. Although the Trademark Bureau is not required to approve licences, a copy of the contract containing the licence must be filed with it and the local SAIC. This is to record that the grant of trademark rights is a temporary licence and not an assignment.

If a Chinese-registered trademark is assigned outright, both the assignor and the assignee must sign an application which must be filed with the Trademark Bureau, together with the original certificate of registration. The assignment will then be noted on the certificate. At this point, the assignee assumes responsibility for the quality of the product produced under the mark. Furthermore, Article 21 of the new Implementing Regulations states that when assigning a trademark, other identical or similar trademarks and identical or similar commodities must be assigned at the same time.

This procedure is different from licensing. Under Chinese law, when licensing a trademark, the licensor always remains responsible for the quality of the goods produced and sold under the mark, even though the trademark has been licensed to someone else. Likewise, the licensor will remain liable to the Chinese public.

DEVELOPING A CHINESE TRADEMARK

An effective product marketing strategy in China depends on a trademark which is effective in Chinese as well as English. A product's trademark must be capable of fast conceptual transmission—the idea sells the product. Therefore, the idea must establish in the consumer's mind a pattern of recognition.

Trademark recognition in the Chinese market depends upon effective use of the Chinese language. In order to promote a Western trademark in the Chinese market, the trademark must retain enough of its original character so that it does not lose its recognition in Western eyes, while at the same time conveying an image that will stick in the minds of Chinese consumers. To do this, one must find an effective combination of Chinese characters.

Adaptability

The goal when adopting a Chinese trademark is to adopt one which can be used in the four major Chinese-language markets: China, Hong Kong, Singapore and Taiwan. The ideal mark should be capable of conceptual translation, so that its conceptual meaning is the same in English, Mandarin and Cantonese. The mark should then be registered in its identical form in China, Hong Kong, Singapore and Taiwan. Where appropriate, it should be registered using both traditional and simplified character forms. The goal should be to develop a standard trademark for trademark protection, whereby marketing strategies and concepts developed for one jurisdiction can later be extended readily to others.

179

Effective Translation

It is often difficult to develop a translation of a new foreign trademark which can be used with equal ease in all three Chinese-speaking markets. It is even more difficult to develop one which supports the marketing strategy of the original mark. Because of the diversity of the marketing strategies required to enter the different Chinese-language markets, there is no single best way of developing a Chinese trademark. If a company entrusts a dozen translators with the translation of its name, they are likely to come up with a dozen different versions because there is no single way to translate any given name into Chinese. Only a few Western translations have been accepted as standard.

Accurate translation has become a very important part of both business and legal work in China. The process of developing a Chinese trademark for a foreign product begins with a basic translation of the foreign mark. There are two ways of translating a foreign trademark:

* the phonetic method known as transliteration, in which characters are used to represent the sound of the foreign word; and

* the conceptual method, whereby characters are used to represent the meaning of the foreign word without regard to the phonetic sound.

Many airline companies have opted for the conceptual method quite successfully. For instance, Northwest Airlines is translated as 'xi bei', which literally means the two directions of north and west; United Airlines is translated as 'lian he', which is an exact translation of the word 'united'; and Flying Tigers is translated as 'fei hu', which literally means flying tiger. These are all very effective translations which retain the original meaning but bear no resemblance to the phonetic sound of the English-language trademark.

On the other hand, the phonetic method of transliteration is often opted for because it best preserves the foreign nature of the product. Transliteration can be an important marketing factor when importing European or American goods into the Chinese market. If the trademark consists of several characters providing an incomprehensible or absurd meaning, the Chinese consumer will immediately recognise it as a transliteration of a foreign trademark. One example of transliteration is the Chinese trademark for Jaguar cars, which in Cantonese is pronounced 'jik gar' and in Mandarin 'ji jia'. These characters mean 'accumulate, frame'. It would be possible to translate Jaguar literally as 'bao', which means 'leopard' or 'jaguar', but the phonetic transliteration was chosen because it automatically evokes the exotic quality of a foreign imported item.

Translation Problems

Chinese is an ancient language, and new characters are not readily introduced. The written language does not, therefore, facilitate the adoption of invented words, which are commonly used in Western trademarks. In Chinese, there are many homonyms and characters with different meanings that have similar, though not identical, pronunciations. This is because spoken Chinese is a tonal language. That is, a single sound can have several meanings depending on the tone of voice in which it is uttered.

In Mandarin, there are four tones. For example, the sound 'ma' means 'mother' in the first tone, 'hemp' in the second tone, 'horse' in the third, 'to curse' in the fourth, and in the neutral tone it indicates that a question has just been asked. Consequently 'ma, ma, ma, ma', using one sound with four different tones, can be a sentence in itself: 'Is mother cursing the horse?' Cantonese is even more complicated because there are nine tones. One must be very careful in speaking Cantonese because sounds used as common expressions when spoken in their correct tone may, in a slightly different tone, form curse words.

Homonyms abound in the Chinese language. For example, there are 38 different characters which are pronounced 'li' in the fourth tone. These characters have a range of meanings as diverse as 'example', 'experience', 'profit', and 'stand'. Translation can be further complicated by the fact that, in Chinese, the same character can have more than one meaning. For instance, the characters 'gong fu' in Mandarin mean 'time'. However, these same characters can also refer to the Chinese martial arts. Therefore, the particular meaning of characters often depends upon the context in which they are spoken or written. The different circumstances in which a character is used become particularly important when translating a Western trademark into Chinese.

Therefore, in the view of the Chinese government, not all homonymous trademarks are similar trademarks. The method used for judging whether homonymous trademarks are similar trademarks is based on the meaning of the words, the visual elements, and whether or not consumers may be misled.

Appropriate Characters for an English Trademark

It is of vital importance when considering the marketing aspects of a product to choose the appropriate character for an English trademark. The problem with phonetic transliteration is that while it can produce sounds that are reasonably close to the original English mark, the meanings of the characters used may be entirely unrelated to the original trademark or product.

Characters producing phonetic sounds similar to an English-language trademark may be meaningless. One example is 'Morgan Stanley', which came out as 'mogen sitanli'. Although this sounds much like the English name, when translated it means literally 'run-root-this-level-benefit', which achieves nothing more than alerting the Chinese to the fact that it is a foreign company. In such cases, the translator should consider abandoning some characters in favour of alternative characters which, although not as close phonetically, convey a more acceptable or desirable meaning. For example, in Hong Kong, the closest phonetic transliteration of 'Panadol' is 'ban lei tuo' meaning 'get ready'. However, simply by changing two characters within the transliteration, the sound 'bi lei tong' is created, which means 'must cure pain'. For marketing purposes, the conceptual association is obviously much better, so these three characters are used instead.

One example of a trademark which both translates and transliterates is the mark used for the Mandarin Hotel in Hong Kong. In Cantonese, it is pronounced 'man hua', which resembles the word 'Mandarin' and literally means 'literate Chinese', an apt description of the elite scholar class of pre-Liberation China.

Probably the most perfect example of a transliteration which is both phonetically accurate and conceptually on target is the translation of 'Coca-Cola'. 'Coca-Cola' is translated into four characters pronounced 'kekou kele', literally meaning 'tasty be happy', or simply 'to quench one's thirst'. The abbreviated 'kele', however, has through popular use become a generic term which, like its English equivalent 'cola', cannot receive individual trademark protection. A trademark with characters like 'kele', which is already generic in China, may be registered provided that one undertakes not to file an objection to Chinese enterprises using the Chinese name.

Simplified characters

From a graphic design point of view, the registration of a foreign trademark in Chinese presents its own set of problems because there are two types of Chinese characters: traditional and simplified. Because it is difficult to write traditional Chinese characters, a new scheme of characters was introduced in 1956, whereby traditional characters were simplified by reducing the number of strokes.

There are, however, many instances where it is still preferable for a Chinese trademark to choose traditional characters instead of their simplified version. From a marketing point of view, traditional characters might be used to suggest a degree of sophistication or a link with the past. On the other hand, some traditional characters are so different from their simplified form that they may not be recognised or understood by people brought up in China's school system, where only the simplified form is taught. Another issue which has emerged in the use of simplified characters is that, despite the fact that the Chinese government has created standard, official simplified characters, people in China and Hong Kong sometimes create their own versions of simplified characters. The result is an array of unofficial simplified characters which create confusion in registering a trademark in China.

When using simplified characters in registering a trademark, it is important to determine whether or not the characters are official. Unfortunately, nothing in China is ever as simple as it seems. The official simplified character list contains many characters which have been adopted only on a trial basis. Consequently, the use of such characters does little to provide the security sought by registering a trademark. Another problem arises from the fact that laws in China are often ambiguous. Having registered a simplified-character trademark, one would reasonably expect the mark to be given equal protection in its traditional character form, and vice versa. (In Hong Kong, registration in one form will automatically protect the other.) Because of the lack of certainty regarding this issue, it is advisable, when registering a trademark in China, to register the characters in both their traditional and simplified forms.

Features of the Chinese language

When selecting the most appropriate Chinese characters for an English trademark, it is important to consider five features of the Chinese language. First, the same characters may yield different sounds in different dialects. For example, the trademark 'Guinness' is translated phonetically in Cantonese as 'Kin Lik Si', meaning 'healthy, energy, scholar'. The same characters in Mandarin are pronounced 'jian li shi', producing sounds which do not resemble the original transliteration of 'Guinness' at all.

Secondly, different Chinese characters often have the same pronunciation. For instance, four completely separate characters which convey four completely different meanings ('family', 'add', 'excellent', and 'furniture') are all pronounced in Cantonese as 'ga' and in mandarin as 'jia'.

Thirdly, some English sounds simply do not exist in Chinese. English words ending in s, r, or l cannot be phonetically translated into Cantonese. Therefore, the translator must overcome the incompatibility of the languages by making up Chinese sounds which are similar to the English ones. This has been done successfully in the case of Dunhill cigarettes. Dunhill is transliterated into Cantonese as 'dun hei lo', which means 'ascend, happiness, road'.

Fourthly, a trademark successfully translated in one dialect may produce undesirable connotations in other dialects. An example of this is the trademark for Skippy peanut butter. In Cantonese, it is pronounced as 'ding ho', meaning 'exceptionally good'. These same Chinese characters (頂好) pronounced in Mandarin, however, sound like 'ding hao', which closely resembles a similar Cantonese sound meaning 'very flirtatious'.

Finally, a phonetic transliteration may produce a strange or absurd meaning. Omega watches is a prime example of this. In Hong Kong, 'Omega' is transliterated as 'ah mi ga', which means 'scream, rice, addition'. Despite this absurd meaning, because of Omega's extensive use, the literal meaning is forgotten, and the characters are associated in people's minds with the Omega brand.

Attempts to create a conceptual translation can produce unique results. For example, Smarties, a sugar-coated chocolate product, is translated in Hong Kong as 'chong meng dou', meaning 'clever beans'. While the conceptual method of translation worked with Smarties, there are many cases where foreign trademarks cannot be translated conceptually at all. An example of this is a stationery brand in Hong Kong called Pentel, which in Chinese has no equivalent conceptual translation whatsoever. Originally it was transliterated phonetically in Cantonese as 'pun tou'. Although this is phonetically a close transliteration of the English trademark 'Pentel', it fails conceptually because in Cantonese the characters used for 'pun tou' translate to mean 'flat peach'. This transliteration was later abandoned and replaced with 'fei long pai', meaning 'flying dragon'. Although the new Chinese trademark sounds nothing like the English trademark 'Pentel', it has more effective connotations for Hong Kong's broad-based Chinese market.

MARKET RECOGNITION OF TRADEMARKS

Some companies that existed in China before 1949 are still known by their pre-Liberation names. Rather than go through the effort of re-inventing the wheel, many of these companies have found it more sensible merely to dust off their old trademarks and put them back into the China market. Citibank is one example of a company which has decided to stick with its old trademark, 'huaqi', which literally means 'flower flag'. (The name was derived from the American flag which once flew over Citibank's old Shanghai office.) Few companies in fact have the option of using pre-Liberation names, but those that do have found a latent brand awareness of their trademark, particularly amongst the older generation.

When translating or transliterating trademark names, the conceptual connotation of a character combination is an important consideration. Because products are often sold only by reference to foreign trademarks, it is easy for Chinese nicknames to become recognised throughout the local market. Such nicknames become common law trademarks through their use in Chinese-language advertising and invoicing. The creation of nicknames is a simple process, being most often derived from the packaging of the products or the shape of the goods. For instance, 'Carnation' in Mandarin has simply become 'sanhua pai', meaning 'three flowers brand', and 'Quaker' has become known as 'laoren pai', meaning, 'old man brand'. The problem with this process is that the nickname by which a product becomes widely known may not be to the liking of the company.

If a trademark application is submitted without a Chinese translation of a Western trademark, the Chinese Trademark Bureau will automatically translate the mark. Once this is done, even if incorrect, it cannot be changed. This creates a problem for a company if its product is already known in the Chinese market under another mark, and the Trademark Bureau designates a translation which bears no relation to it. In addition, the translation given by the Trademark Bureau may not always evoke the image which the company wants to promote. This is precisely what happened with the Mercedes Benz mark. The popular Chinese trademark for Mercedes Benz was 'benshi', meaning 'heading for speed'. Because Mercedes Benz is internationally famous, the Chinese translation 'benshi' had long been in popular use in China. Unfortunately, when the company submitted its trademark application for Mercedes Benz, it did not submit its own Chinese translation, so the Trademark Office decided to give the trademark a new translation. Instead of 'benshi', it translated 'Mercedes Benz' as 'benci', which has the absurd meaning of 'basic, thatch'.

The Chinese say that 'once given a bad name, it can never be washed off'. Consequently, an undesirable nickname that has been used extensively in the Chinese-language market becomes difficult to disassociate from the actual name of the company to which it has been applied. The only solution is to launch an advertising campaign aimed at transferring the trademark name. This provides no guaranteed result, and may prove to be time-consuming and costly.

This same kind of problem can occur in describing the product. If a company registering its trademark fails to submit a Chinese translation of the product description, the Trademark Bureau will fill in its own translation. The possibility of an incorrect translation is fairly high resulting in inadequate protection which defeats the purpose of registering a trademark. In one instance, a chemical company submitted two applications without the Chinese translation of the relevant products. In the first case, it wrote in English that the trademark was to be used for 'herbicides'. The Trademark Bureau filled in the characters 'chuyouji, zhiwu shengzhang tiaojieji', which means 'herbicides, and preparations for regulating the growth of plants'—actually giving, through mistranslation, the product more protection than it was applying for. The same company also submitted an application in which the goods were described as 'synthetic resins and plastics in extruded form'. This time, the Trademark Bureau translation, 'hecheng shuzhi he jiya chengxing de suliao', meant 'synthetic resins and extruded form plastic materials'. This had the effect of limiting the scope of protection intended for the product in the original trademark application.

CONCLUSION

It is essential to take full control of Chinese-language communications as soon as possible when entering the Chinese market. This means using a newly developed trademark right from the very first sale. Counsel experienced in translation and the cultural subtleties of the Chinese market should be consulted.

Every year, hundreds of millions of dollars are spent in Asia to correct marketing problems resulting from negligence in planning and developing accurate and effective Chinese versions of foreign trademarks. China, with its vast disparities in regional dialects, is a market that continues to develop. Great care will be needed in planning and translating foreign trademarks for products being introduced to China.

CHAPTER 19

PATENTS

If China is to achieve the Four Modernisations, it must have advanced technology. However, investors are not always willing to transfer their technology to China due to fears that their ownership rights to the technology will not be protected. Only when technology is protected will investors be willing to supply China with what it needs to achieve its modernisation goals.

When *The Patent Law of the People's Republic of China* (the Patent Law) was introduced in 1985 it provided protection for investors willing to apply for patent rights in China. Unlike the concept of trademarks, or even copyright, patent protection is relatively new to China. There is no earlier legislation on patents or recognised patent rights in either China's ancient or modern history.

THE PATENT OFFICE

The China Patent Office was established before the enactment of the Patent Law. This might seem strange, given that the Patent Law should be what regulates the activities of the Patent Office. Nevertheless, the Chinese government wanted to have the Patent Office functioning by the time that law was enacted so that patent applications could be handled without delay once the law had been promulgated.

The Patent Office, established under the State Science and Technology Commission, is the government body authorised to manage and administer patent-related matters, and is the only body which may accept and examine patent applications and grant patent registrations for 'invention–creation'. It may also formulate regulations for the protection of patent rights and supervise the actual enforcement of these regulations. Additionally, it coordinates international cooperation for the protection of intellectual property.

The Patent Office has domestic and foreign sections. In total, there are 5000 patent offices, of which 4600 provide domestic services and the remainder service foreigners. Six service divisions— administrative, mechanical, electrical, chemical, application service and legal services—review and file patent applications, and provide consultancy and translation services. It institutes proceedings in infringement cases, and handles matters involving objections and requests for the invalidation of a patent right.

PATENT LEGISLATION

The Patent Law was adopted at the Fourth Session of the Standing Committee of the Sixth National People's Congress on 12 March 1984. It came into force on 1 April 1985. It protects both domestic and foreign inventions provided that the inventors have applied for patent protection in China. The Patent Law establishes the right to patent protection for inventions and creations defined as inventions, utility models and designs. It was amended by the National People's Congress in 1992.

In August 1984 the Notification on Setting up Administrative Authorities for Patent Affairs throughout the Country was issued with the approval of the State Council, the State Economic Commission, the State Science and Technology Commission, the Ministry of Labour and Personnel and the Patent Office. This notification called for the establishment of patent-administration divisions by all provinces, autonomous regions and municipalities under the State Council. In addition, ministries, commissions and bureaus under the State Council, as well as Special Economic Zones and Open Cities, were permitted to establish patent-administration divisions. The notification also provided for the establishment and improvement of patent-service facilities, as well as the establishment of patent-service units in provinces, autonomous regions and municipalities under the State Council.

The Detailed Rules and Regulations for the Implementation of the Patent Law were promulgated on 19 January 1985 by the Patent Office after approval by the State Council. They specify the details required in the application for a patent and the conditions under which patent rights may be invalidated. Licences may be granted upon the expiration of a patent, and rewards made to the inventor or creator of an 'invention–creation'.

The regulations also provide for fees and give general information concerning the adjudication of disputes. The Patent Office maintains a patent register of new patent rights granted as well as the assignment of such rights.

CHINA'S MEMBERSHIP OF INTERNATIONAL CONVENTIONS

China has also acceded to the Paris Convention for the Protection of Industrial Property 1883. In March 1985, it became the ninety-sixth signatory to the Paris Convention, which has enabled it to receive foreign patent applications and to file patent applications abroad since the Patent Law was implemented.

In relation to disputes arising over patent rights, two pieces of legislation have been promulgated. The Patent Administration Authorities Adjudicating Patent Dispute Procedures went into effect on 4 December 1989. These provided for the adjudication of disputes involving infringements through mediation by the Patent Administrative Authorities in the locality where the dispute arises. The Patent Office Administrative Review Rules, promulgated on 29 December 1991 by the Patent Office, provide for the review of administrative measures concerning disputes or infringements. On 15 September 1993, China acceded to the Patent Cooperation Treaty. The Patent Office deals with cases involving the Treaty, conducting international patent searches and preliminary examinations.

TAIWAN PATENTS

The Patent Office announced special regulations for patent applications from the province of Taiwan in January 1988, making it easier for Taiwan compatriots to apply for patents. It is hoped that this will encourage technical exchanges across the Straits. Under the regulations, Taiwan compatriots will be protected by China's Patent Law; in other words, Taiwan compatriots will enjoy the same treatment as other persons in China. They may apply directly for patent rights, or ask patent agents in China to help them complete the procedures. To ensure smooth communication with applicants, the Patent Office has proposed that Taiwan applicants communicate with the Patent Office through friends or relatives in China. If applicants do not have contacts in China, they can go through the China Patent Agent (HK) Ltd. The term 'China Taiwan' must be used in the applications, and not the erroneous term 'Republic of China'.

CONCLUSION

When the Patent Law was introduced to protect both domestic and foreign inventions, little did anyone realise that it would spark an invention boom. Between April 1985 and the end of March 1988, the China Patent Office received 66,599 patent applications, of which 15,350 were from foreigners. Domestic applications are usually for design and utility models; these take less than a year to be tested and officially approved. It is interesting to note that most domestic applications for patent rights involve technology which China needs in order to develop its agricultural, forestry, animal husbandry, fishery, and electronics industries. Foreign applications, however, focus on technology related to computers, semiconductors, and information storage.

CHAPTER 20

COPYRIGHT

Of the three recognised forms of intellectual property law in China—trademarks, patents and copyright—the law of copyright took the longest to develop. The Chinese authorities promulgated the Trademark Law in 1983 and, two years later, introduced the Patent Law.

Why did China take so long to develop a copyright law when it has moved with great efficiency in developing legislation to protect both trademarks and patents? The delay may be due to some extent to previous national policies regarding artistic expression. During the Cultural Revolution, all forms of artistic and literary expression were reduced to expressions of State ideology. From a socialist viewpoint, an author's work is a product of his mental labour. During the Cultural Revolution, such mental labour was considered to be without value. Following the Cultural Revolution, however, books and music began to be published again in greater quantity.

DEVELOPMENT OF COPYRIGHT PROTECTION

China's first copyright law, the Copyright Law of the Great Qing Empire, was promulgated in 1910. Ironically, the Qing Dynasty used Japanese law as the basis for its first copyright law. However, it did not last for long. With the liberation of China in 1949, the Qing Copyright Law was abolished.

While the new government of the People's Republic of China planned to develop a copyright law of its own, the country had other priorities. Emphasis was placed on development and national construction, and the promulgation of a copyright law was pushed aside. Political changes and the Anti-Rightist Campaign then resulted in the concept of copyright being associated with the intellectual class, and progress on the law was once again delayed.

At this point, however, a new socialist culture was developing in

China, creating in the process the need to provide protection so as to encourage authors in their creative work. Such protection was carried out through individual government departments, which formulated their own regulations.

The General Principles of Civil Law (the 'Civil Law'), promulgated in China on 1 January 1985, permitted citizens of China to enjoy copyright protection. Article 94 of the Civil Law states: 'Citizens enjoy the author's right (copyright), and are entitled by law to the rights, signing, publishing, printing and obtaining remuneration for their works'. This created an immediate problem. Although people had the expectation of copyright, there existed no formalised national copyright law to effect such protection. This resulted in an increasing number of copyright disputes being taken to court.

In 1979, the issue of formulating a national copyright law for China arose for the first time. The initial draft of the Copyright Law was produced in 1980, followed by constant amendments. Finally, *The Copyright Law of the People's Republic of China* (the Copyright Law) was adopted by the National People's Congress on 7 September 1990, thereby establishing the basic principles of protection for an author's published and unpublished works. This was followed shortly thereafter by the Regulations for the Implementation of the Copyright Law of the People's Republic of China, promulgated on 1 June 1991 by the State Council.

On 5 July 1994, the Punishment of Crimes of Copyright Infringement was adopted at the Eighth Session of the Standing Committee of the Eighth National People's Congress of the People's Republic of China. This provision is added to the Criminal Law to punish crimes of copyright infringement and to protect copyright-related rights and interests. Regulations on Computer Software Protection were promulgated by the State Council on 4 June 1994. In October of that year, Regulations on Administration of Audio-visual Products were promulgated.

COPYRIGHT LAW FOR AUTHORS

After Liberation, China adopted a socialist system and a State-planned economy. Authors were salaried employees of the State and therefore had little incentive to produce much. Furthermore, artistic creations could be used by the State on more than one occasion. Because the authors were on fixed salaries, they could not expect to receive commensurate remuneration for republication of their works. After the Cultural Revolution, and with the gradual decentralisation of the economy, authors became more independent and even began to work freelance. Although most authors remain State-salaried employees, many have joined authors' societies or associations on a contractual basis, while others have left State research institutions to form research groups of their own.

When all authors worked for the State at a fixed salary, the concept of copyright protection was largely irrelevant. Now, however, copyright has taken on a new importance within China's changing economy because, without copyright protection, the incomes of independent groups and individuals may be threatened.

CHINA'S MEMBERSHIP OF INTERNATIONAL CONVENTIONS

In 1980, China joined the World Intellectual Property Organisation (WIPO), an agency of UNESCO. Hong Kong, because it is presently still occupied by British colonialists, now receives protection through the United Kingdom, which is a member of the Berne Convention and the Universal Copyright Convention. Works from convention countries are protected in all other member countries.

After 1997, works in Hong Kong will be protected throughout the world, because Hong Kong will have been returned to China, which has recently joined the Berne Convention, following the adoption of its own Copyright Law. Furthermore, on 4 January 1993, the Chinese government presented its instrument of accession to the Convention for the Protection of Producers of Phonograms Against Unauthorized Duplication of Their Phonograms to WIPO, and became a member state as of 30 April 1993.

DEVELOPMENT OF NATIONAL COPYRIGHT ADMINISTRATION

The State Copyright Administration, which reports directly to the State Council, was established in 1985. Its function is to promote and enforce the rights attached to the concept of copyright. The Copyright

Administration consists of five departments: copyright, legal, internal, information and documentation, and a general office.

Most provinces, autonomous regions and municipalities have now set up their own administrative authorities for copyright to ensure that the rights and interests of intellectuals are protected. These bodies are responsible for:

- implementing the relevant State regulations on the protection of copyright;
- training copyright managerial personnel; and
- handling copyright disputes.

In 1988, two more copyright organisations were established in China. The China Copyright Agent Corporation provides a registration service for authors. Registration of authorship is not compulsory in China; rather, the registration system was introduced as a means by which authors could establish proof of authorship in the event that an infringement should occur. In addition, a law firm was established in Beijing to handle disputes involving copyright issues. Foreigners who feel that their rights have been infringed can ask this firm to act on their behalf.

The following bodies are responsible for overseeing matters related to copyright.

- The National Administration for Copyright (NAC) is the administrative body established under the State Science and Technology Commission (SSTC) responsible for supervising issues relating to copyright and formulates legislation. It authorises the use of copyright works and issues licences for the reprinting and translation of foreign works. It is also the body responsible for handling copyright disputes.

- The State Science and Technology Commission (SSTC) formulates general policy matters related to computer software technology.

- The Ministry of Machinery and Electronics Industry (MMEI) has been granted supervisory authority over issues related to copyright registration and protection for computer software. The Computer Software Review Commission and China Computer Software Registration Centre (described below) are established under MMEI to carry out this work.

- The Computer Software Review Commission (CSRC) is established under the administration of MMEI and is the body in charge of the review of applications for the registration of copyrights for computer software. The CSRC comprises experts from the legal profession as well as experts on computer software technology, who carry out the actual review of applications received.

- The China Computer Software Registration Centre (CCSRC) has been charged by MMEI with responsibility for the actual registration of computer software following review by the CSRC.

CONCLUSION

China's intellectual property legislation has always been aimed at providing adequate protection for foreign investors in order to safeguard their investments and encourage technology transfer. Without adequate legislative protection of copyright, foreigners would be reluctant to provide forms of technical know-how.

CHAPTER 21

TECHNOLOGY TRANSFER

Technology transfer in China is often identified as being the importation of anything which is an improvement upon existing technology (which in China is often outdated by international standards). Technology transfer legislation in China is applicable to agreements or contracts involving the transfer of patented technology, production, production processes, and technical or management know-how. At the national level, there are several key pieces of legislation governing contracts for the importation of technology. Under this legislation, the Ministry of Foreign Trade and Economic Cooperation (MOFTEC) is granted a wide degree of policy discretion in approving technology import contracts.

TECHNOLOGY IMPORT CONTRACT REGULATIONS

The Provisional Rules for the Transfer of Technology were adopted by the State Council on 10 January 1985. The Regulations on the Administration of Technology Import Contracts (the Technology Import Contract Regulations) were promulgated by the State Council on 24 May 1985. The importation of technology is defined as:

- the assignment or licensing of patent or other industrial property rights;
- the licensing of know-how; or
- the transfer of technical services.

The regulations require imported technology to be both 'advanced and appropriate'. To qualify, the technology must:

- be capable of developing new products;
- improve upon the quality and performance of existing products; or
- reduce production costs.

The regulations apply when transferring or licensing technology to China. Technology import contracts involving the transfer of patent or trademark rights are also governed by the regulations, provided that the patents and trademarks concerned have obtained protection in China. The patent or application numbers and trademark registration numbers must be specified in the application. By supplying the number, the recipient is able to verify and confirm the patent and trademark right as well as its duration.

Implementation of the Regulations

The Detailed Rules for the Implementation of the Regulations on the Administration of Technology Import Contracts (the Technology Contract Implementing Rules) were promulgated by MOFTEC on 20 January 1988, replacing the earlier Procedures for the Examination and Approval of Technology Import Contracts. The new rules define five types of contract for which MOFTEC's approval is mandatory:

(1) contracts for the assignment or licensing of industrial property rights;

(2) contracts for technical services;

(3) contracts for cooperative production or cooperative designs involving the assignment or licensing of industrial property rights or the licensing of know-how or technical services;

(4) contracts for the importation of complete sets of equipment and production lines, and key equipment involving the assignment or licensing of industrial property rights, the licensing of know-how or technical services; and

(5) other technology import contracts which the examination and approval authorities believe should undergo procedures for examination and approval.

Contract Terms

The Technology Import Contract Regulations are administered by MOFTEC. Contracts subject to them must be submitted for approval to MOFTEC or to bodies authorised by MOFTEC, within 30 days of signature. MOFTEC will either approve or reject the contract within 60 days of receipt of the application. The contract will automatically go into effect upon approval. If MOFTEC or the approving authority fails to respond to the application within 60 days, the contract may be considered approved.

The Technology Contract Implementing Rules clarify in detail the terms which should be included in a technology import contract and the approval process. Furthermore, they set out certain conditions under which MOFTEC will not grant approval. Approval will not be granted if a contract:

- violates State laws and regulations;
- is not consistent with the original feasibility study;
- contains 'unreasonable' prices for imported equipment;
- is harmful to the public interest and the sovereign rights of the State; or
- fails to provide quality guarantees for products manufactured with the technology being transferred.

The provisions of the Implementing Rules also place restrictions on the activities that are permissible in a technology import contract. These provisions cover activities such as:

- price fixing;
- restricting export sales;
- restricting the use of technology after expiration of the contract; and
- restricting the party receiving the technology from continuing to purchase parts and components from the seller, and the payment of royalties on expired patents.

These create a problem for sellers who may wish to ensure that the Chinese buyer uses hardware designed for software products and vice versa, as the Implementing Rules allow the Chinese party to purchase products by other manufacturers and prevent any contractual restrictions on this. Enforceability of this clause under the legislation is ineffective in respect of patent issues unless such patent has been properly registered under Chinese law. The actual enforceability of any obligation to maintain confidentiality of information will be subject to a variety of factors in China, not always under the full control of the receiver of the information or know-how concerned.

Technology import contracts involving the transfer of patent rights must be filed with the Patent Office. Likewise, contracts involving trademarks must be filed with the Trademark Bureau. In the case of trademarks, a specimen must also be attached. According to Article 15 involved in the transferred technology has not expired, then 'the matter shall be handled in accordance with the relevant provisions of the Patent Law of the People's Republic of China'. In other words, if the contract has expired and the patent has not, the contract must be extended in order that the technology may continue to be used.

IMPORTATION OF KNOW-HOW AND TECHNOLOGY

The Interim Provisions for Encouraging the Import of Know-how (the Interim Provisions) were promulgated by the State Council to provide a policy initiative to all ministries under the State Council and their offices at each locality, and to encourage such offices to include the importation of know-how in their economic plans. The Interim Provisions state that all planning departments must select 'technology or know-how import projects' as part of their plans, and reflect current national policy in giving priority to projects involving the importation of know-how and technology. Tax exemptions and reductions are recommended, as well as encouraging Chinese banks to provide financing for such projects.

Starting in 1984, a number of cities in China promulgated their own local legislation for the importation of technology. Much of this legislation preceded the national level legislation described above. The legislation promulgated in the Special Economic Zones may be viewed as experimental in light of the national legislation which has followed (which to some extent is very similar to the local legislation).

Questions often arise when there is a conflict between the terms of the local legislation and national legislation as to which should apply, if the contract applies to a locality where local legislation has been promulgated. The interpretation most often agreed upon is that the national legislation overrides the local legislation except where the local legislation addresses issues not addressed in the national legislation.

CONCLUSION

The protection of technology has become an increasingly important issue for foreign investors, particularly as the demands of the China market call for increasingly advanced technology for production purposes. China further encourages technology transfer through its general policies on foreign investment.

It is therefore crucial for foreign investors to pay careful attention to the legislation in relation to technology transfer, and to obtain concrete approval of all such technology transfer contracts.

APPENDICES

CHINA FOREIGN INVESTMENT GUIDELINES CATALOGUE (BY SECTOR IN 1995)

INVESTMENTS ENCOURAGED

Projects in agriculture, infrastructure, primary industrial materials, hi-tech and energy conservation, as well as environmental protection. Investment in north-west China is also encouraged.

(1) Agriculture/Forestry/Fishing/Animal Husbandry

- developing barren land and mountains;
- new varieties of cotton, oils, sugar, vegetables, flowers and grasses;
- cultivating imported tree varieties;
- animal breeding;
- producing pesticides, high-concentration fertiliser, plastic greenhouse materials, livestock vaccinations and hormones, and chemicals for forestry;
- construction/operation of large hydropower and water-supply systems (State must have a controlling share); and
- farming equipment.

(2) Light Industry

- non-metal products;
- commercial paper pulp;
- leather processing;
- hi-tech batteries;
- industrial sewing machines;
- plastic wrap for food;
- enzyme detergents;
- synthetic scents; and
- substitutes for freon used in automobiles.

(3) Textiles

- special fabrics (e.g. fire-resistant or non-conductive);
- printing on fabrics;
- oils used in producing fabrics; and
- special textiles for industry.

(4) Transportation/Telecommunications

- railway equipment and technology, major parts of trains, railway lines;
- equipment for high-speed trains, signals and safety equipment;
- construction/operation of local railways (no wholly foreign ownership allowed), bridges (no wholly foreign ownership allowed), tunnels (no wholly foreign ownership allowed) and ferries (no wholly foreign ownership allowed);
- port and road building equipment;
- construction/operation of city underground (State must have a controlling share), light railways (State must have a controlling share), roads (State must have a controlling share), bridges (State must have a controlling share), tunnels (State must have a controlling share), ports (State must have a controlling share) and civilian airports (State must have a controlling share);
- producing digital mobile-telecommunications equipment; and
- producing optical-cable microwave telecommunications systems.

(5) Coal

- design/manufacturing of drills and excavators;
- producing high-grade additives for the coal industry; and
- developing cool-burning coal and by-products.

(6) Power

construction/operation of thermal power stations (State must have a controlling share), large hydroelectric power stations (State must have a controlling share), nuclear power stations (State must have a controlling share), and alternative energy power stations (e.g. solar, wind, magnetism, tidal power).

(7) Ferrous Metals

- sponge iron;
- powder metallurgy; and
- large steel-production lines.

(8) Non-ferrous Metals

- hard alloys and tin-related products;
- compounds made from non-ferrous metals;
- mining of copper (no wholly foreign ownership allowed), tin (no wholly foreign ownership allowed), lead (no wholly foreign ownership allowed), and aluminum (no wholly foreign ownership allowed); and
- application of rare earth.

(9) Petrochemicals

- large-scale production of ethylene and propylene;
- engineering plastics and plastic compounds;
- synthetic rubber;
- fine petrochemicals including those for making paper, processing leather;
- chlorine powder;
- chemical products from coal;
- comprehensive use of waste gas, waste liquid and waste solids; and
- construction/operation of oil, gas and petrochemical port terminals (State must have a controlling share).

(10) Machinery

- robotic soldering and welding tools;
- heat-resistant materials;
- heavy rolling mills and related equipment;
- equipment for moving coal out of mines; and
- cargo-loading cranes.

(11) Electronics

- large-scale production of integrated circuits;
- optical components; and
- powerful computers.

(12) Building and Non-Metal Materials

- large glass factories, toilet-production facilities;
- new building materials;
- special cement, cement additives, cement transport equipment;
- tunnel-digging machines; and
- other precision machinery.

(13) Pharmaceuticals/Medical Equipment

- items protected by Chinese patents;
- anti-inflammatories;
- drugs for heart disease;
- new drug packaging material; and
- X-ray machines, electrocardiograms.

(14) Aerospace/Aeronautics

civilian planes, engines used in aviation industry, electronics.

(15) Ship Building

special-purpose ships and related hardware.

(16) Emerging Industries

- microelectronic technology;
- information and telecommunications technology;
- ocean development technology; and
- energy-saving, recycling and pollution clean-up technology.

(17) Services

- international economy and technology consulting services; and
- after-sales service for precision equipment.

INVESTMENTS SUBJECT TO RESTRICTIONS

These are areas for which the technology has already been imported and domestic capacity is already sufficient. It also includes the service sector, where foreign involvement is being tried on an experimental basis.

Category A : Approval at Provincial Level

- producing sedans, light vans, motorcycles, auto engines;
- producing thermal and nuclear power equipment;
- producing colour television sets, colour picture tubes and glass shells, video cameras, VCRs;
- program-controlled switchboard equipment;
- building trunk railroads; and
- operating water transport and cross-border road transport.

Category B : Approval at Ministry Level

- air transport;
- general-purpose aviation;
- retail and wholesale business;
- materials supply and marketing;
- foreign trade;
- banking, insurance, securities, accounting, auditing, legal-counselling services; and
- mining/smelting/processing of precious ores and precious minerals.

Note: Project proposal must be approved by the relevant ministry under the State Council. Feasibility study must be approved at the provincial level and reported to the State Planning Commission or the State Economics and Trade Commission.

INVESTMENTS PROHIBITED

Projects that harm State security or the public interest, threaten the environment or public health, use large amounts of arable land, breach the security of military facilities or that employ traditional Chinese methods.

(1) Agriculture/Fishing/Forestry

- protected animals and plants;
- rare animals and plants;
- setting up business in nature reserves; and
- growing/processing green tea and other special teas.

(2) Light Industry

- processing ivory and tiger balm;
- producing hand-made carpets;
- certain traditional painting and ceramics; and
- traditional art papers and ink.

(3) Power/Public Works

setting up/operating electrical transmission network or city water, gas or heating-supply network.

(4) Mining

mining and processing of radioactive materials.

(5) Pharmaceuticals

- Chinese herbs on the national protection list; and
- processing herbs by traditional Chinese methods.

(6) Posts/Telecommunications/Transportation

- operation of postal and telecommunications businesses; and
- air-traffic control.

(7) Trading

futures trading.

(8) Broadcasting/Movie Industry

- operation of television, radio and cable broadcast stations and relay stations;

- production/publication/distribution of radio and TV programs and films; and
- broadcasting video tapes.

(9) News Media

(10) Military Weapons Production

(11) Other

- projects that breach military security and functioning;
- processing undertakings that might cause cancer or other diseases;
- horse-racing tracks and gambling; and
- prostitution.

SAMPLE CONTRACT FOR JOINT VENTURES USING CHINESE AND FOREIGN INVESTMENT

CHAPTER 1 : GENERAL PROVISIONS

In accordance with *The Law of the People's Republic of China on Joint Ventures Using Chinese and Foreign Investment* and other relevant Chinese laws and regulations, _____ Company and _____ Company, adhering to the principle of equality and mutual benefit and through friendly consultations, agree to jointly invest to set up a joint venture enterprise in _____ the People's Republic of China. The contract hereunder is worked out.

CHAPTER 2 : PARTIES TO THE JOINT VENTURE

Article 1

Parties of this contract are as follows: _____ Company (hereinafter referred to as Party A), registered with _____ in China, and its legal address is at _____ (street) _____ (district) _____ (city) _____ China.

Legal representative: Name:
                       Position:
                       Nationality:

_____ Company (hereinafter referred to as Party B), registered with _____. Its legal address at _____:

Legal representative: Name:
                       Position:
                       Nationality:

(**Note:** In case there are more than two investors, they will be called party C, D... in sequence.)

CHAPTER 3: ESTABLISHMENT OF THE JOINT VENTURE COMPANY

Article 2

In accordance with *The Law of the People's Republic of China on Joint Ventures Using Chinese and Foreign Investment* and other relevant Chinese laws and regulations, both parties of the joint venture agree to set up _____ joint venture limited liability company (hereinafter referred to as the joint venture company).

Article 3

The name of the joint venture company is _____ Limited Liability Company.

The name in foreign language is _____.

The legal address of the joint venture company is at _____ (street) _____ (city) _____ (province).

Article 4

All activities of the joint venture company shall be governed by the laws, decrees and pertinent rules and regulations of the People's Republic of China.

Article 5

The organisation form of the joint venture company is a limited liability company. Each party to the joint venture company is liable to the joint venture company within the limit of the capital subscribed by it. The profits, risks and losses of the joint venture company shall be shared by the parties in proportion to their contributions of the registered capital.

CHAPTER 4: THE PURPOSE, SCOPE AND SCALE OF PRODUCTION AND BUSINESS

Article 6

The purpose of the parties to the joint venture is in conformity with the wish of enhancing economic cooperation and technical exchanges, to improve the product quality, develop new products, and gain competitive position in the world market in quality and price by adopting advanced and appropriate technology and scientific management method, so as to raise economic output and ensure satisfactory economic benefits for each investor.

(**Note:** This article may be written according to the specific requirements of the contract.)

Article 7

The productive and business scope of the joint venture company is to produce _____ products; provide maintenance service after the sale of the products; and study and develop new products.

(**Note:** This can be written in the contract according to the specific requirements.)

Article 8

The production outputs of the joint venture company are as follows:

1. The production capacity after the joint venture goes into operation is _____.

2. Output may be increased up to _____ with the development of the production and operation. The product varieties may be developed into _____.

(**Note:** This may be written according to the situation.)

CHAPTER 5 : TOTAL AMOUNT OF INVESTMENT AND THE REGISTERED CAPITAL

Article 9

The total amount of investment of the joint venture company is RMB _____ (or a foreign currency agreed upon by both parties).

Article 10

Investment contributed by the parties is RMB _____, which will be the registered capital of the joint venture company.

Of which: Party A shall pay _____ Yuan, accounts for _____%; Party B shall pay _____ Yuan, accounts for _____%.

Article 11

Both Party A and Party B will contribute the following as their investment:

Party A: cash _____ Yuan
machines and equipment _____ Yuan
premises _____ Yuan
the right to the use of the site _____ Yuan
Other _____ Yuan, _____ Yuan in total

Party B: cash _____ Yuan
machines and equipment _____ Yuan
industrial property _____ Yuan
the right to the use of the site _____ Yuan
Other _____ Yuan, _____ Yuan in total

(**Note:** When contributing capital goods or industrial property as investment, Party A and Party B should conclude a separate agreement to be a schedule to this main contract.)

Article 12

The registered capital of the joint venture company shall be paid in _____ instalments by Party A and Party B according to the respective proportion of their investment.

Each instalment shall be as follows:

(**Note:** This may be written according to the actual conditions.)

Article 13

In case any party to the joint venture intends to assign all or part of his investment subscribed to a third party, consent shall be obtained from the other party to the joint venture, and approval from the examination and approval authority is required.

When one party to the joint venture assigns all or part of his investment, the other party has pre-emptive right.

CHAPTER 6 : RESPONSIBILITIES OF EACH PARTY TO THE JOINT VENTURE

Article 14

Party A and Party B shall be responsible for the following matters.

Responsibilities of Party A:

- handling of applications for approval, registration, business licence and other matters concerning the establishment of the joint venture company with the relevant departments in charge in China;
- processing the application for the right to the use of a site with the authority in charge of the land;
- organising the design and construction of the premises and other engineering facilities of the joint venture company;
- providing cash, machinery and equipment and premises...in accordance with the stipulations in Article 11;
- assisting Party B to process import customs declarations for the machinery and equipment contributed by Party B as investment and arranging the transportation within China;
- assisting the joint venture company in purchasing or leasing equipment, materials, raw materials, articles for office use, means of transportation and communication facilities, etc.;
- assisting the joint venture company in contracting and settling fundamental facilities such as water, electricity and transportation;
- assisting the joint venture in recruiting Chinese management personnel, technical personnel, workers and other personnel needed;
- assisting foreign workers and staff in applying for entry visas, work licences and processing their travel arrangements; and
- other matters entrusted by the joint venture company.

Responsibilities of Party B:

- providing cash, machinery and equipment, industrial property...in accordance with the stipulations in Article 11, and shipping capital goods such as machinery and equipment contributed as investment to a Chinese port;

- handling matters entrusted by the joint venture company such as selecting and purchasing machinery and equipment outside China;

- providing technical personnel for installing, testing and trialling the equipment, as well as the technical personnel for production and inspection;

- training technical personnel and workers of the joint venture company;

- if Party B is the licensor, ensuring the stable production of approved products of the joint venture company according to design capacity within the stipulated period; and

- other matters entrusted by the joint venture company.

(**Note:** The above may be written according to the specific situation.)

CHAPTER 7 : TRANSFER OF TECHNOLOGY

Article 15

Both Party A and Party B agree that a technology transfer agreement shall be signed between the joint venture company and Party B (or a third party) so as to obtain the advanced technology needed for production and operational purposes and to meet the production output stipulated in Chapter 4 of the contract, including product design, technology of manufacture, means of testing, materials prescription, standard of quality and the training of personnel, etc.

(**Note:** The above may be written in the contract according to the actual conditions.)

Article 16

Party B offers the following guarantees on the transfer of technology. (**Note:** This article applies only when Party B is responsible for transferring technology to the joint venture company.)

1. Party B guarantees that the overall technology such as the design, technology of manufacture, technological process, tests and inspection of products (**Note:** The names of the products must be in writing) provided to the joint venture company is integrated, precise and reliable. It must meet the requirements of the joint venture's operation, and be capable of reaching the standard of production quality and production capacity stipulated in the contract.

2. Party B guarantees that the technology stipulated in this contract and the technology transfer agreement shall be fully transferred to the joint venture company, and pledges that the technology provided is of an advanced standard and meets the criteria expected of it by Party B, and that the model, specifications and quality of the equipment are excellent and meet the technological needs of the operation.

3. Party B shall work out a detailed list of the technology and technological service to be provided at various stages as stipulated in the technology transfer agreement, to be an appendix to the contract, and to guarantee its performance.

4. The drawings, technological specifications and other detailed information are part of the transferred technology and shall be supplied on time.

5. Within the validity period of the technology transfer agreement, Party B shall provide the joint venture company with any improvement on the technology, and the relevant information and technological materials will be supplied quickly and at no additional cost.

6. Party B shall guarantee that the technological personnel and the workers in the joint venture company can master all the technology transferred within the period stipulated in the technology transfer agreement.

Article 17

In case Party B fails to provide equipment and technology in accordance with the stipulations in this contract and in the technology transfer agreement or if any deceiving or concealing actions are found, Party B shall be responsible for compensating the joint venture company for the consequent losses.

Article 18

The technology transfer fee shall be paid in royalties. The royalty rate shall be _____% of the net sales value of the products manufactured.

The term of royalty payment is the same as the term of the technology transfer agreement stipulated in Article 19 of this contract.

Article 19

The term of the technology transfer agreement signed by the joint venture company and Party B is _____ years. After the expiration of the technology transfer agreement, the joint venture company shall have the right to use, research and develop the imported technology continuously. (**Note:** The term for a technology transfer agreement is generally no longer than 10 years, and it must be approved by the Ministry of Foreign Economic Relations and Trade or other examination and approval authorities entrusted by the Ministry of Foreign Economic Relations and Trade.)

CHAPTER 8 : SELLING OF PRODUCTS

Article 20

The products of the joint venture company will be sold on both the Chinese market and overseas: the export part accounts for _____%, _____% for domestic market.

(**Note:** An annual percentage and amount for overseas and domestic sales will be written out according to practical situations; in normal conditions, the amount for export shall at least meet the foreign exchange needs of the joint venture company.)

Article 21

Products may be sold overseas through the following channels:

- The joint venture company may directly sell its products on the international market, which accounts for _____%.
- The joint venture company may sign sales contracts with Chinese foreign trade companies, entrusting them to be the sales agencies or exclusive sales agencies, which accounts for _____%.

- The joint venture company may entrust Party B to sell its products, which accounts for _____%.

Article 22

The joint venture's products to be sold in China may be handled by the Chinese materials and commercial departments by means of agency or exclusive sales, or may be sold by the joint venture company directly.

Article 23

In order to provide a maintenance service for the products sold both in China or abroad, the joint venture company may set up sales branches for maintenance both in China or abroad subject to the approval of the relative Chinese department.

Article 24

The trademark of the joint venture's product is _____.

CHAPTER 9: THE BOARD OF DIRECTORS

Article 25

The date of registration of the joint venture company shall be the date of the establishment of the board of directors of the joint venture company.

Article 26

The board of directors is composed of _____ directors, of which _____ shall be appointed by Party A, _____ by Party B. The chairman of the board shall be appointed by Party A, and its vice-chairman by Party B. The term of office for the directors, chairman and vice-chairman is four years; their terms of office may be renewed if continuously appointed by the relevant party.

Article 27

The highest authority of the joint venture company shall be its board of directors. It shall decide all major issues (**Note:** The main contents shall be listed according to Article 36 of the Regulations for the

Implementation of the Joint Venture Law) concerning the joint venture company. Unanimous approval shall be required before any decisions are made concerning major issues. As for other matters, approval by a simple majority shall be required. (**Note:** This must be explicitly stipulated in the contract.)

Article 28

The chairman of the board is the legal representative of the joint venture company. Should the chairman be unable to exercise his responsibilities for some reason, he shall authorise the vice-chairman or any other director to represent the joint venture company temporarily.

Article 29

The board of directors shall convene at least once every year. The meeting shall be called and presided over by the chairman of the board. The chairman may convene an interim meeting at the request of over a third of the total number of directors. Minutes of the meetings shall be placed on file.

CHAPTER 10 : BUSINESS MANAGEMENT OFFICE

Article 30

The joint venture company shall establish a management office which shall be responsible for its daily management. The management office shall have a general manager, appointed by party _____; _____ deputy general managers, _____ by party _____; _____ by party _____. The general manager and deputy general managers shall be appointed by the board of directors for a term of _____ years.

Article 31

The responsibility of the general manager is to carry out the decisions taken at board meetings and organise and conduct the daily management of the joint venture company. The deputy general managers shall assist the general manager in his work.

Several department managers may be appointed by the management office. They shall be responsible for the work in their respective departments, handle the matters handed over by the general manager and deputy general managers and shall be responsible to them.

Article 32

In case of graft or serious dereliction of duty on the part of the general manager and deputy general managers, the board of directors shall have the power to dismiss them at any time.

CHAPTER 11: PURCHASE OF EQUIPMENT

Article 33

In its purchase of required raw materials, fuel, parts, means of transportation and articles for office use, etc., the joint venture company shall give first priority to purchase in China where conditions are the same.

Article 34

In case the joint venture company entrusts Party B to purchase equipment on an overseas market, persons appointed by Party A shall be invited to take part in the purchasing.

CHAPTER 12: PREPARATION AND CONSTRUCTION

Article 35

During the period of preparation and construction, a preparation and construction office shall be set up under the board of directors. The preparation and construction office shall consist of _____ persons, among which _____ persons will be from Party A, _____ persons from Party B. The preparation and construction office shall have one manager recommended by Party _____, and one deputy manager by Party _____. The manager and deputy manager shall be appointed by the board of directors.

Article 36

The preparation and construction office is responsible for the following specific work: examining the designs of the project, signing project construction contracts, organising the purchase and inspection of equipment, materials, etc., working out the general schedule of project construction, compiling the expenditure plans, controlling financial payments and final accounts of the project, drawing up managerial methods and keeping and compiling documents, drawings, files and materials, etc., during the construction period of the project.

Article 37

A technical group with several technical personnel appointed by Party A and Party B shall be organised. The group, under the leadership of the preparation and construction office, is in charge of the examination, supervision, inspection, testing, checking and accepting, and performance checking for the project design, the quality of the project, the equipment and materials and the imported technology.

Article 38

After approval by both parties, the establishment, remuneration and the expenses of the staff of the preparation and construction office shall be covered in the project budget.

Article 39

After completing the project and finishing the turning over procedures, the preparation and construction office shall be dissolved upon the approval of the board of directors.

CHAPTER 13: LABOUR MANAGEMENT

Article 40

Labour contracts covering the recruitment, employment, dismissal and resignation, wages, labour insurance, welfare, rewards, penalties and other matters concerning the staff and workers of the joint venture company shall be drawn up between the joint venture company and the trade union of the joint venture company as a whole or for individual employees in accordance with the Regulations of the People's Republic of China on Labour Management in Joint Ventures using Chinese and Foreign Investment, and its Implementation Rules.

The labour contracts shall, after being signed, be filed with the local labour management department.

Article 41

The appointment of high-ranking administrative personnel recommended by both parties, their salaries, social insurance, welfare and the level of travelling expenses, etc., shall be decided at a meeting of the board of directors.

CHAPTER 14: TAXES, FINANCE AND AUDIT

Article 42

The joint venture company shall pay taxes in accordance with the stipulations of Chinese laws and other relevant regulations.

Article 43

Staff members and workers of the joint venture company shall pay individual income tax according to *The Individual Income Tax Law of the People's Republic of China.*

Article 44

Allocations for reserve funds, expansion funds of the joint venture company and welfare funds and bonuses for staff and workers shall be set aside in accordance with the stipulations in *The Law of the People's Republic of China on Joint Ventures using Chinese and Foreign Investment.* The annual proportion of allocations shall be decided by the board of directors according to the business situation of the joint venture company.

Article 45

The fiscal year of the joint venture company shall be from 1 January to 31 December. All vouchers, receipts, statistical statements and reports, and account books shall be written in Chinese. (**Note:** A foreign language can be used concurrently with mutual consent.)

Article 46

Financial checking and examination of the joint venture company shall be conducted by an auditor registered in China and reports shall be submitted to the board of directors and the general manager.

In case Party B considers it necessary to employ a foreign auditor registered in another country to undertake annual financial checking and examination, Party A shall give its consent. All the expenses thereof shall be borne by Party B.

Article 47

In the first three months of each fiscal year, the manager shall prepare the previous year's balance sheet, profit and loss statement and proposal regarding the disposal of profits, and submit them to the board of directors for examination and approval.

CHAPTER 15 : DURATION OF THE JOINT VENTURE

Article 48

The duration of the joint venture company is _____ years. The establishment of the joint venture company shall start from the date on which the business licence of the joint venture company is issued.

An application for the extension of the duration, proposed by one party and unanimously approved by the board of directors, shall be submitted to the Ministry of Foreign Economic Relations and Trade (or the examination and approval authority entrusted by it) six months prior to the expiry date of the joint venture.

CHAPTER 16 : THE DISPOSAL OF ASSETS AFTER THE EXPIRATION OF THE DURATION

Article 49

Upon the expiration of the duration or termination before the date of expiration of the joint venture, liquidation shall be carried out according to the relevant law. The liquidated assets shall be distributed in accordance with the proportion of investment contributed by Party A and Party B.

CHAPTER 17 : INSURANCE

Article 50

Insurance policies of the joint venture company on various kinds of risk shall be underwritten with the People's Republic of China. Types, the value and duration of insurance shall be decided by the board of directors in accordance with the stipulations of the People's Insurance Company of China.

CHAPTER 18 : THE AMENDMENT, ALTERATION AND DISCHARGE OF THE CONTRACT

Article 51

An amendment of the contract or its appendices shall come into force only after the written agreement to it has been signed by Party A and Party B and it has been approved by the original examination and approval authority.

Article 52

In case of inability to fulfil the contract or to continue operations due to heavy losses in successive years as a result of *force majeure,* the duration of the joint venture and the contract shall be terminated before the time of expiration after the unanimous agreement of the board of directors and approval by the original examination and approval authority.

Article 53

Should the joint venture company be unable to continue its operations or achieve the business purpose stipulated in the contract due to the fact that one of the contracting parties fails to fulfil the obligations prescribed by the contract and articles of association, or seriously violates the stipulations of the contract and articles of association, that party shall be deemed to have unilaterally terminated the contract. The other party shall have the right to terminate the contract in accordance with the provisions of the contract after obtaining the approval of the original examination and approval authority, as well as to claim damages. If Party A and Party B of the joint venture company agree to continue the operation, the party that fails to fulfil its obligations shall be liable for the economic losses thus caused to the joint venture company.

CHAPTER 19 : LIABILITIES FOR BREACH OF CONTRACT

Article 54

Should either Party A or Party B fail to pay on schedule the contributions in accordance with the provisions defined in Chapter 5 of this contract, the defaulting party shall pay to the other party _____% of the contribution starting from the first month following the expiration of the time-limit. Should the defaulting party fail to pay after three months, _____% of the contribution shall be paid to the other party, who shall have the right to terminate the contract and to claim damages from the defaulting party in accordance with the stipulations in Article 53 of the contract.

Article 55

Should all or part of the contract and its appendices be unable to be fulfilled owing to the fault of one party, that party shall bear the responsibilities resulting. Should it be the fault of both parties, they shall bear their respective responsibilities according to the actual situation.

Article 56

In order to guarantee the performance of the contract and its appendices, both Party A and Party B shall provide each other with bank guarantees for the performance of the contract.

CHAPTER 20 : *FORCE MAJEURE*

Article 57

Should either of the parties to the contract be prevented from executing the contract by *force majeure,* such as earthquake, typhoon, flood, fire and war and other unforeseen events, and their occurrence and consequences are unpreventable and unavoidable, the affected party shall notify the other party by cable or facsimile message without delay, and within 15 days thereafter provide the detailed information of the events and a valid document as evidence issued by the relevant public notary organisation to explain the reason for its inability to execute or for having to delay the execution of all or part of the contract. Both parties shall, through consultations, decide whether to terminate the contract or to exempt the relevant obligations for implementation of the contract, or whether to delay the execution of the contract until the effects of the events affecting the performance of the contract can be better assessed.

CHAPTER 21 : APPLICABLE LAW

Article 58

The formation of this contract, its validity, interpretation, execution and settlement of disputes shall be governed by the related laws of the People's Republic of China.

CHAPTER 22: SETTLEMENT OF DISPUTES

Article 59

Any disputes arising from the execution of, or in connection with, the contract shall be settled through friendly consultations between both parities. In case no settlement can be reached through consultations, the disputes shall be submitted to the Foreign Economic and Trade Arbitration Commission of the China Council for the Promotion of International Trade for arbitration in accordance with its rules of procedure. The arbitral award is final and binding upon both parties.
　OR
Any disputes arising from the execution of, or in connection with, the contract shall be settled through friendly consultations between both parties. If no settlement can be reached through consultations, the disputes shall be submitted to _____ Arbitration Organisation in _____ for arbitration in accordance with its rules of procedure. The arbital award is final and binding upon both parties.
　OR

Any disputes arising from the execution of, or in connection with, the contract shall be settled through friendly consultations between both parties. If no settlement can be reached through consultations, the disputes shall be submitted for arbitration. Arbitration shall take place in the defendant's country.

If in China, arbitration shall be conducted by the Foreign Economic and Trade Arbitration Commission of the China Council for the Promotion of International Trade in accordance with its rules of procedure.

If in _____, the arbitration shall be conducted by _____ in accordance with its rules of procedure.

The arbitral award is final and binding on both parties.

(**Note:** When formulating contracts, only one of the above-mentioned provisions can be used.)

Article 60

During the arbitration, the contract shall continue to be executed by both parties except for those matters in dispute.

CHAPTER 23 : LANGUAGE

Article 61

The contract shall be written in Chinese and in _____. Both languages are equally valid. In the event of any discrepancy between the two versions, the Chinese version shall prevail.

CHAPTER 24 : EFFECTIVENESS OF THE CONTRACT AND MISCELLANEOUS ISSUES

Article 62

The appendices drawn up in accordance with the principles of this contract are an integral part of it, including the project agreement, the technology transfer agreement, the sales agreement...

Article 63

The contract and its appendices shall come into force from the date of approval by the Ministry of Foreign Economic Relations and Trade of the People's Republic of China (or its entrusted examination and approval authority).

Article 64

Should notices in connection with any party's rights and obligations be sent by either Party A or Party B by telegram, telex or facsimile message, the written notices shall be also required afterwards. The legal addresses of Party A and Party B listed in this contract shall be the postal addresses.

Article 65

The contract is signed in _____, of China by the authorised representatives of both parties on _____ 19____.

For Party A   For Party B
(Signature)   (Signature)

SAMPLE ARTICLES OF ASSOCIATION FOR JOINT VENTURES USING CHINESE AND FOREIGN INVESTMENT

CHAPTER 1 : GENERAL PROVISIONS

Article 1

In accordance with *The Law of the People's Republic of China on Joint Ventures using Chinese and Foreign Investment* and the contract signed by _____ company (hereinafter referred to as Party A) and _____ company (hereinafter referred to as Party B), the articles of association are hereby formulated.

Article 2

The name of the joint venture company shall be _____ Limited Liability Company.

Its name in foreign language is _____.

The legal address of the joint venture company is at _____.

Article 3

The names and legal addresses of the parties to the joint venture are as follows:

Party A: _____ Company at _____.
Party B: _____ Company at _____.

Article 4

The joint venture company is a limited liability company.

Article 5

The joint venture company has the status of a legal entity and is subject to the jurisdiction and protection of China's laws concerned.

All its activities shall be governed by Chinese laws, decrees and other pertinent rules and regulations.

CHAPTER 2 : PURPOSE AND SCOPE OF BUSINESS

Article 6

The purpose of the joint venture company is to produce and sell _____ products and to obtain satisfactory economic benefits for the parties to the joint venture company. (**Note:** Each joint venture company completes this Article according to its particular circumstances.)

Article 7

The business scope of the joint venture company is to design, manufacture and sell _____ products and provide aftersales services.

Article 8

The scale of production of the joint venture company is as follows:

_____ year _____ (unit of quantity)

_____ year _____

_____ year _____

Article 9

The joint venture company may sell its products on the Chinese domestic market and on the international market. The proportions are as follows:

_____ (year): _____ % for export

_____ % for the domestic market

_____ (year): _____ % for export

_____ % for the domestic market

(**Note:** The marketing methods and obligations will be stipulated according to actual conditions.)

CHAPTER 3 : THE TOTAL AMOUNT OF INVESTMENT AND THE REGISTERED CAPITAL

Article 10

The total amount of investment of the joint venture company is RMB_____.

Article 11

The investment contributed by each party is as follows:

Party A: Investment subscribed is RMB_____, which accounts for _____% of the registered capital. It includes:

Cash _____
Machinery and equipment _____
Premises _____
Land use right _____
Industrial property _____
Other _____

Party B: Investment subscribed is RMB_____, which accounts for _____% of the registered capital. It includes:

Cash _____
Machinery and equipment _____
Industrial property _____
Other _____

Article 12

The parties to the joint venture shall pay in all the investment subscribed according to the time-limit stipulated in the contract.

Article 13

After the investment is paid by the parties to the joint venture, a Chinese-registered accountant invited by the joint venture company shall verify it and provide a certificate of verification. According to this certificate, the joint venture shall issue an investment certificate which included the following items: name of the joint venture; date of the establishment of the joint venture; names of the parties and the investment contributed; date of the contribution of the investment, and the date of issuance of the investment certificate.

Article 14

During the term of the joint venture, the joint venture company shall not reduce its registered capital.

Article 15

Should one party assign all or part of its investment subscribed, consent shall be obtained from the other party to the joint venture. When one party assigns its investment, the other party has pre-emptive right.

Article 16

Any increase or assignment of the registered capital of the joint venture company shall be approved by the board of directors and submitted to the original examination and approval authority for approval. The registration procedures for changes shall be dealt with at the original registration and administration office.

CHAPTER 4 : THE BOARD OF DIRECTORS

Article 17

The joint venture shall establish the board of directors which is the highest authority of the joint venture company.

Article 18

The board of directors shall decide all major issues concerning the joint venture company. Its functions and powers are as follows:

- deciding and approving important reports submitted by the general manager (for instance, production plan, annual business report, funds, loans, etc.);
- approving annual financial reports, budget of receipts and expenditures, distribution plan of annual profits;
- adopting major rules and regulations of the company;
- deciding to set up branches;

- amending the articles of association of the company;
- discussing and deciding the termination of production, termination of the company or merging with another economic organisation;
- deciding the engagement of senior personnel such as the general manager, chief engineer, treasurer, auditor, etc.;
- being in charge of the winding-up of the company and other liquidation matters upon the expiration of the joint venture company; and
- other major issues which shall be decided by the board of directors.

Article 19

The board of directors shall consist of _____ directors, of which _____ shall be appointed by Party A and _____ by Party B. The term of office for the directors is four years and may be renewed.

Article 20

The chairman of the board shall be appointed by Party A and the vice-chairman of the board by Party B.

Article 21

When appointing and replacing directors, a written notice shall be submitted to the board.

Article 22

The board of directors shall convene _____ meeting(s) every year. An interim meeting of the board of directors may be held at the request of over a third of the total number of directors.

Article 23

Board meetings will normally be held at the principal offices of the company.

Article 24

Board meetings shall be called and presided over by the chairman.

Should the chairman be absent, the vice-chairman shall call and preside over the board meeting.

Article 25

The chairman shall give each director a written notice of a board meeting 30 days before the date of the board meeting. The notice shall cover the agenda, time and place of the meeting.

Article 26

Should a director be unable to attend a board meeting, he may present a proxy in written form to the board. If a director neither attends nor entrusts another to attend the meeting, he will be regarded as abstaining.

Article 27

A board meeting requires a quorum of over two-thirds of the total number of directors. When the quorum is less than two-thirds, the decisions adopted by the board meeting are invalid.

Article 28

Detailed written records shall be made of each board meeting and signed by all the directors in attendance or by their appointed proxies. The records shall be in Chinese and _____, and shall be filed with the company.

Article 29

The following issues shall be unanimously agreed upon by the board of directors.

(**Note:** These issues should be stipulated according to each company's actual situation.)

Article 30

The following issues shall be passed by over [   ] of the total number of directors.

(**Note:** The actual proportion is determined by the parties to the contract.)

CHAPTER 5 : BUSINESS MANAGEMENT ORGANISATION

Article 31

The joint venture company shall establish a management organisation. It should consist of production, technology, marketing, finance and administration offices, etc. (**Note:** This Article should be completed according to each company's actual situation.)

Article 32

The joint venture company shall have one general manager and _____ deputy general manager(s) who are engaged by the board of directors. The first general manager shall be recommended by party _____; the deputy general manager(s) by party _____.

Article 33

The general manager is directly responsible to the board of directors. He shall carry out the decisions of the board of directors, and organise and conduct the daily production and technical operation and management of the joint venture company. The deputy general managers shall assist the general manager in his work and act as the agent of the general manager during his absence and exercise the functions of the general manager.

Article 34

Decisions on the major issues concerning the daily work of the joint venture company shall be signed jointly by the general manager and deputy general managers; then the decisions shall come into effect. Issues which need co-signatures shall be specifically stipulated by the board of directors.

Article 35

The terms of office for the general manager and deputy general managers shall be _____ years, and may be renewed at the invitation of the board of directors.

Article 36

At the invitation of the board of directors, the chairman, vice-chairman or directors of the board may concurrently be the general manager, deputy general managers or other high-ranking personnel of the joint venture company.

Article 37

The general manager or deputy general managers shall not hold posts concurrently as general manager or deputy general managers of other economic organisations in commercial competition with their own joint venture company.

Article 38

The joint venture company shall have one chief engineer, one treasurer and one auditor engaged by the board of directors.

Article 39

The general engineer, treasurer and auditor shall be under the supervision of the general manager.

The treasurer shall supervise the financial and accounting affairs, organise the joint venture company's overall business accounting and be responsible for systems for the economic running of the business.

The auditor shall be in charge of the auditing work of the joint venture company, examine and check the financial receipts and expenditure and the accounts, and submit written reports to the general manager and the board of directors.

Article 40

The general manager, deputy general managers, chief engineer, treasurer, auditor and other high-ranking personnel who wish to resign must submit their written resignations to the board of directors in advance.

In case any one of the above-mentioned persons engages in graft or commits a serious dereliction of duty, they may be dismissed at any time upon the decision of the board. Those who violate the criminal law shall be liable to criminal sanction.

CHAPTER 6: FINANCE AND ACCOUNTING

Article 41

The finances and accounting of the joint venture company shall be handled in accordance with the Stipulations of the Finance and Accounting System of the Joint Ventures using Chinese and Foreign Investment formulated by the Ministry of Finance of the People's Republic of China.

Article 42

The fiscal year of the joint venture company shall coincide with the calendar year, i.e. from 1 January to 31 December on the Gregorian calendar.

Article 43

All vouchers, account books, statistical statements and reports of the joint venture company shall be written in Chinese.

Article 44

The joint venture company adopts Renminbi as its accounts-keeping currency. The conversion of Renminbi into other currency shall be in accordance with the exchange rate published by the State Administration of Exchange Control of the People's Republic of China on the date of conversion.

Article 45

The joint venture company shall open accounts in Renminbi and foreign currency with the Bank of China or other banks agreed by the Bank of China.

Article 46

The accounting systems of the joint venture company shall adopt the internationally used accrual basis and debit and credit accounting methods.

Article 47

The following items shall be covered in the financial accounts books:

(1) the amount of overall cash receipts and expenses of the joint venture company;

(2) all material purchasing and selling of the joint venture company;

(3) the registered capital and debts situation of the joint venture company; and

(4) the time of payment, increase and assignment of the registered capital of the joint venture company.

Article 48

The joint venture company shall work out the statement of assets and liabilities and losses and gains accounts of the past year in the first three months of each fiscal year, and submit them to a board meeting for approval after being examined and signed by the auditor.

Article 49

Parties to the joint venture have the right to invite an auditor to undertake annual financial checks and examinations at their own expense. The joint venture company shall provide facilities for the checking and examination.

Article 50

The depreciation period for the fixed assets of the joint venture company shall be decided by the board of directors in accordance with the Rules for the Implementation of the Income Tax Law of the People's Republic of China Concerning Joint Ventures with Chinese and Foreign Investment.

Article 51

All matters concerning foreign exchange shall be handled in accordance with the Provisional Regulations for Exchange Control of the People's Republic of China, and other pertaining regulations as well as the stipulations of the joint venture contract.

CHAPTER 7 : PROFIT SHARING

Article 52

The joint venture company shall draw reserve funds, expansion funds and bonus welfare funds for staff and workers after payment of taxes. The proportion of allocation is decided by the board of directors.

Article 53

After paying the taxes in accordance with the law and drawing the various funds, the remaining profits will be distributed according to the proportion of each party's investment in the registered capital.

Article 54

The joint venture company shall distribute its profits. The profit distribution plan and the amount of profit distributed to each party shall be published within the first three months following each fiscal year.

Article 55

The joint venture company shall not distribute profits unless the losses of the previous fiscal year have been made up. Remaining profits from previous years can be distributed together with that of the current year.

CHAPTER 8 : STAFF AND WORKERS

Article 56

The employment, recruitment, dismissal and resignation of the staff and workers of the joint venture company and their salaries, welfare benefits, labour insurance, labour protection, labour discipline and other matters shall be handled according to the Regulations of the People's Republic of China on Labour Management in Joint Ventures using Chinese and Foreign Investment and its implementation rules.

Article 57

The staff and workers to be recruited by the joint venture company will be recommended by the local labour department or the joint venture will do so through public selection examinations and employ those who are qualified with the consent of the labour department.

Article 58

The joint venture company has the right to take disciplinary actions, record a demerit and reduce the salaries of those staff and workers who violate the rules and regulations of the joint venture company. Those with serious cases may be dismissed. Discharge of workers shall be filed with the labour and personnel department in the locality.

Article 59

The salary levels of the staff and workers shall be set by the board of directors according to the specific situation of the joint venture, with reference to the relevant stipulations of China, and shall be specified in detail in the labour contract.

The salary of the staff and workers shall be increased correspondingly with the development of production and advances in the ability and technology of the staff and workers.

Article 60

Matters concerning welfare funds, bonuses, labour protection and labour insurance, etc., shall be stipulated respectively in various rules by the joint venture company, to ensure that the staff and workers work under proper conditions.

CHAPTER 9 : THE TRADE UNION ORGANISATION

Article 61

The staff and workers of the joint venture company have the right to establish trade union organisations and carry out activities in accordance with the stipulations of *The Trade Union Law of the People's Republic of China*.

Article 62

The trade union in the joint venture company is representative of the interests of the staff and workers. The tasks of the trade union are to protect the democratic rights and material interests of the staff and workers pursuant to the law; to assist the joint venture company to arrange and make rational use of welfare funds and bonuses; to organise political, professional, scientific and technical studies, and carry out literary, art and sports activities; and to educate staff and workers to observe labour discipline and strive to fulfil the economic tasks of the joint venture company.

Article 63

The trade union of the joint venture company will sign labour contracts with the joint venture company on behalf of the staff and workers, and supervise the implementation of the contracts.

Article 64

Persons in charge of the trade union of the joint venture company have the right to attend as non-voting members and to report the opinions and demands of staff and workers to meetings of the board of directors held to discuss issues such as development plans, production and operational activities of the joint venture.

Article 65

The trade union shall take part in the mediation of disputes arising between the staff and workers and the joint venture company.

Article 66

The joint venture company shall allot an amount of money totally 2% of all the salaries of the staff and workers of the joint venture company as the trade union's funds, which shall be used by the trade union in accordance with the Managerial Rules for the Trade Union Funds formulated by the All China Federation of Trade Unions.

CHAPTER 10 : DURATION, TERMINATION AND LIQUIDATION

Article 67

The duration of the joint venture company shall be _____ years, beginning from the day when the business license is issued.

Article 68

An application for the extension of duration shall be proposed by both parties and approved at a board meeting, and be submitted to the original examination and approval authority six months prior to the expiry date of the joint venture. Only upon approval may the duration be extended, and the joint venture company shall go through registration formalities for alteration at the original registration office.

Article 69

The joint venture may be terminated before its expiration if the parties to the joint venture agree unanimously that the termination of the joint venture is in the best interests of the parties.

The decision to terminate the joint venture before the term expires shall be taken by the board of directors through a plenary meeting, and shall be submitted to the original examination and approval authority for approval.

Article 70

Either party shall have the right to terminate the joint venture in the event one of the following situations occurs.

(**Note:** Situations should be stipulated according to each joint venture company's actual circumstances.)

Article 71

Upon the expiration or termination of the joint venture before its term ends, the board of directors shall work out procedures and principles for the liquidation, nominate candidates for the liquidation committee and set up the liquidation committee to liquidate the joint venture company's assets.

Article 72

The tasks of the liquidation committee are: to conduct a thorough check of the property of the joint venture company, the claims upon it and its indebtedness; to work out the statement of assets and liabilities and list of property; and to formulate a liquidation plan. All these tasks shall be carried out upon the approval of the board of directors.

Article 73

During the process of liquidation, the liquidation committee shall represent the company to sue and be sued.

Article 74

The liquidation expenses and remuneration of the members of the liquidation committee shall take priority in payment from the existing assets of the joint venture company.

Article 75

The remaining property after the clearance of the debts of the joint venture company shall be distributed among the parties to the joint venture according to the proportion of each party's investment in the registered capital.

Article 76

On completion of the liquidation, the joint venture company shall submit a liquidation report to the original examination and approval authority, go through the formalities for nullifying its registration in the original registration office and hand in its business licence. At the same time, it shall make an announcement to the public.

Article 77

After the winding-up of the joint venture company, its books of account shall be left in the care of the Chinese participant.

CHAPTER 11 : RULES AND REGULATIONS

Article 78

Following are the rules and regulations formulated by the board of directors of the joint venture company:

(1) management regulations, including the powers and functions of the managerial branches and its working rules and procedures;

(2) rules for the staff and workers;

(3) system of labour and salary;

(4) system of work attendance records, promotions and awards and penalties for the staff and workers;

(5) detailed rules of staff and workers welfare;

(6) financial system;

(7) liquidation procedures upon the dissolution of the joint venture company; and

(8) other necessary rules and regulations.

CHAPTER 12 : SUPPLEMENTARY ARTICLES

Article 79

The amendments to the articles of association shall be unanimously agreed and decided by the board of directors and submitted to the original examination and approval authority for approval.

Article 80

The articles of association are written in the Chinese language and _____ language. Both languages shall be equally valid. In the event of any discrepancy between the two above-mentioned versions, the Chinese version shall prevail.

Article 81

The articles of association shall come into effect upon the approval of the Ministry of Foreign Economic Relations and Trade of the People's Republic of China (or its entrusted examination and approval authority). The same applies in the event of amendments.

Article 82

The articles of association are signed in _____ of China by the authorised representatives of both parties on _____ 19____.

For Party A   For Party B
(Signature)   (Signature)

SAMPLE APPLICATION FOR THE ESTABLISHMENT OF A FOREIGN CAPITAL ENTERPRISE IN CHINA

APPLICATION FORM FOR THE ESTABLISHMENT OF A FOREIGN CAPITAL ENTERPRISE IN CHINA

Information concerning the company applying for the establishment of a foreign capital enterprise (hereinafter the company):

1. Name of the company: _____

2. Legal Address: _____

3. Country or Jurisdiction of Incorporation: _____

   _____

4. Date of Incorporation: _____

5. Name of the Legal Representative: _____

   Nationality: _____

6. Business Scope: _____

7. Scale of Production: _____

8. Total Assets: _____

9. Registered Capital: _____

10. Bank: _____

11. Countries Where Investment Has Been Made: _____

    _____

    _____

    _____

12. Attach Balance Sheets for the past 3 years. If the company has less than 3 years of operations, attach information for parent company.

13. Name of the Contact Person for the Company in China.

 Address: _____

 Telephone Number: _____

The Foreign Capital Enterprise to be established in China

1. Name of the Foreign Capital Enterprise: _____

 _____

2. Address: _____

3. Total Amount of Investment: _____

4. Amount of Registered Capital: _____

5. The Foreign Capital Enterprise shall be a limited liability company. Liability shall be limited to _____ (Amount of registered capital)

6. Form of Investment:

 a. Foreign Currency: _____

 b. Equipment: _____

 c. Technology: _____

 d. Other: _____

7. Land Surface Area and Building Surface Area Needed: _____

 _____

 a. Office: _____

 b. Manufacturing: _____

 c. Other Buildings: _____

8. Project Conditions:

 a. Scope: _____

 b. Production Scale: _____

 c. Raw Materials and Their Sources: _____

 d. Sources of Machine Fittings: _____

 e. Product Uses: _____

   f. Market for Sales: _____

   g. Export Ratio: _____

   h. Plan for the Balancing of Foreign Exchange Expenditures and Receipts (Please attach)

9. Management of the Foreign Capital Enterprise

   a. Composition of the Board of Directors: _____

      _____

      _____

   b. Management Offices and Senior Staff: _____

      _____

   c. System of Financial Affairs and Accounting: _____

      _____

   d. Total Staff and Workers: _____

      Foreign Staff and Workers: _____

      Management Personnel: _____

      Technical Personnel: _____

      Workers: _____

10. Department in Charge: _____

Construction and Implementation of the Project

1. Technology to be used in carrying out the project:

   _____

   _____

2. Machinery and equipment to be used for the project:

   _____

   _____

3. The volume of water, electricity, gas, fuel, etc. which will be needed by the project: _____

   _____

4. The standard of the treatment of "Three Wastes" and the security standard: _____

_____

5. Schedule of Planned Construction:

Year 1: _____

Year 2: _____

6. Starting Date for Production: _____

7. Quantity of Products Planned in the First Three Years of Production:

a. Year 1: _____

b. Year 2: _____

c. Year 3: _____

8. Principal Raw Materials to be Purchased in China:

a. Year 1: _____

b. Year 2: _____

c. Year 3: _____

9. Raw Materials to be Imported:

a. Year 1: _____

b. Year 2: _____

c. Year 3: _____

10. Plan for the Training of Chinese Staff and Workers:

_____

_____

_____

_____

Term of Operation of the Foreign Capital Enterprise

The Company Hereby Agrees to the Following Conditions for the Establishment of the Foreign Capital Enterprise:

1. All activities of the foreign capital enterprise shall comply with and be protected by the laws, decrees, and relevant regulations of the People's Republic of China.

2. The foreign capital enterprise shall pay the relevant taxes in accordance with the laws, decrees and relevant regulations of the People's Republic of China.

Company:

_____

By:

_____

Legal Representative:

_____

Attachments

1. Articles of Association of the Foreign Capital Enterprise

2. Evidence of Incorporation of the Company

3. Notarised Power of Attorney in favour of the Legal Representative of the Investing Company

4. Balance Sheets for the Past Three Years of Operation of the Investing Company

5. Plan for the Balancing of Foreign Exchange Expenditures and Receipts

SAMPLE APPROVAL CERTIFICATES FOR A FOREIGN INVESTMENT ENTERPRISE

People's Republic of China

Foreign Investment Application

Certificate of Approval

Ref No:

Date: _____

TYPE ONE

NO.

Name of Corporation	Chinese	南翔纺织有限公司		
	English	Nan Xiang Textile Co. Ltd.		
Address		25, Triple Circle West Rd, Beijing, China.		
Nature of Business		Joint Venture	**Years of Tenure**	20 Yrs
Name of Corporation & Places of Incorporation		A. China Textile Co B. Beijing Garment Pte Ltd C. Hong Kong Nan Tai Co. Ltd	PRC PRC Hong Kong	
Total Investment		20 million HK$		
Authorised Captial		20 million HK$		
Shareholding & Capital Commitment		A. China Textile Co B. Beijing Garment Pte Ltd C. Hong Kong Nan Tai Co. Ltd	3 million RMB Plant & Existing Facility 1.16 million HK$	21% 21% 58%
Main Business Activity		1. Production of all types of garments. 2. Research & development of new technology. 3. Fashion design.		

TYPE TWO

Certificate of Approval for Foreign Investment Corporation

DUPLICATE

NO.

Name of Corporation	Chinese	南翔纺织有限公司		
	English	Nan Xiang Textile Co. Ltd.		
Address		25, Triple Circle West Rd, Beijing, China.		
Postal Code		100066	**Telephone**	4016631
Nature of Business		Joint Venture	**Years of Tenure**	20 Yrs
Name of Corporation & Places of Incorporation		A. China Textile Co B. Beijing Garment Pte Ltd C. Hong Kong Nan Tai Co. Ltd		PRC PRC Hong Kong
Total Investment		HK$20 million	**in US$**	US$2.58 million
Authorised Captial		HK$20 million	**in US$**	US$2.58 million
Shareholding & Capital Commitment		A. China Textile Co	3 million RMB	21%
		B. Beijing Garment Pte Ltd	Plant & Existing Facility	21%
		C. Hong Kong Nan Tai Co. Ltd	1.16 million HK$	58%
Main Business Activity		1. Production of all types of garments. 2. Research & development of new technology. 3. Fashion design.		

Issued by: _____

Approved by: _____

Approval Ref: _____

Date: _____

257

INDEX